TYPE 2 DIABETES COOKBOOK FOR BEGINNERS

365 Days Simple & Quick Recipes with Inexpensive Ingredients to Lower Your Blood Sugar for Diabetics and Pre-Diabetics | Bonus: 28 Days Healthy Meal Plan

NATHAN TERRELL

TABLE OF CONTENTS

Introduction

Diabetes is a common disease which leads to metabolic disorders of carbohydrates and water balance.

As a result of that, the pancreatic functions are impaired. It is the pancreas that produces an important hormone called insulin.

Insulin regulates the level of blood sugar that is supplied with food. Without it, the body cannot convert sugar into glucose, and sugar starts accumulating in the body of a person with the disease.

Apart from the pancreas disorders, the water balance is impaired as well. As a result of that, the tissues do not retain water, and the kidneys excrete much fluid.

So what happens when a person has diabetes?

When the condition develops, the body produces too little insulin. At the same time, the level of blood sugar increases and the cells become starved for glucose, which is the main base of energy.

Types Of Diabetes

There are two types of diabetes.

Type 1 diabetes. This condition is also known as insulin-dependent. It usually affects young people under 40. Individuals with type 1 diabetes will need to take insulin injections for the rest of their lives because their body produces antibodies that destroy the beta-cells which produce the hormone.

Type 1 diabetes is hard to cure. However, it is possible to restore pancreatic functions by adhering to a healthy diet. Products with a high glycemic index such as soda, juice and sweets should be excluded.

Type 2 diabetes. this happens as a result of lack of sensitivity of the pancreas cells towards insulin because of the excess of nutrients. People with excess weight are the most susceptible to the disease.

Symptoms & Risk factors

In type 1 diabetes, the list of symptoms can be extensive with both serious and less obvious indicators. Below, I will list the most common symptoms as well as other potential complications of type 1 diabetes:

- **Excessive thirst:** Extreme thirst is one of the less noticeable indicators of type 1 diabetes. It is brought upon by high blood sugar (hyperglycemia).

- **Frequent urination:** Frequent urination is caused by your kidneys failing to process all of the glucose in your blood; this forces your body to attempt to flush out excess glucose through urinating.

- **Fatigue:** Fatigue in type 1 diabetes patients is caused by the body's inability to process glucose for energy.

- **Excessive hunger:** Those suffering from type 1 diabetes often have persistent hunger and increased appetites. This is because the body is desperate for glucose despite its inability to process it without insulin.

- **Cloudy or unclear vision:** Rapid fluctuations in blood sugar levels can lead to cloudy or blurred vision. Those suffering from untreated type 1 diabetes are unable to naturally control their blood sugar levels, making rapid fluctuations a very common occurrence.

- **Rapid weight loss:** Rapid weight loss is probably the most noticeable symptom of type 1 diabetes. As your body starves off glucose, it resorts to breaking down muscle and fat to sustain itself. This can lead to incredibly fast weight loss in type 1 diabetes cases.

- **Ketoacidosis:** Ketoacidosis is a potentially deadly complication of untreated type 1 diabetes. In response to the lack of glucose being fed into your muscles and organs, your body starts breaking down your fat and muscle into an energy source called ketones, which can be burned without the need of insulin. Ketones are usually perfectly fine in normal amounts. But, when your body is starving, it may end up flooding itself with ketones in an attempt to fuel itself; the acidification of your blood that follows this influx of acid molecules may lead to more serious conditions, a coma, or death.

In cases of type 2 diabetes, the symptoms tend to be slower to develop, and they tend to be mild early on. Some early symptoms mimic type 1 diabetes and may include:

- **Excessive hunger:** Similar to type 1 diabetes, those of us with type 2 diabetes will feel constant hunger. Again, this is brought on by our bodies looking for fuel because of our inability to process glucose.

- **Fatigue and mental fog:** Depending on the severity of the insulin shortage in type 2 sufferers, they may feel physical fatigue and a mental fogginess during their average day.

- **Frequent urination:** Another symptom of both type 1 and 2 diabetes. Frequent urination is simply your body's way of attempting to rid itself of excess glucose.

- **Dry mouth and constant thirst:** It are unclear what causes dry mouth in diabetic sufferers, but it is tightly linked to high blood sugar levels. Constant thirst is brought on not only by a dry mouth but also by the dehydration that frequent urination causes.

- **Itchy skin:** Itching of the skin, especially around the hands and feet, is a sign of polyneuropathy (diabetic nerve damage). As well as being a sign of potential nerve damage, itching can be a sign of high concentrations of cytokines circulating in your bloodstream; these are inflammatory molecules that can lead to itching. Cytokines are signaling proteins and hormonal regulators that are often released in high amounts before nerve damage.

SYMPTOMS OF TYPE 2 DIABETES

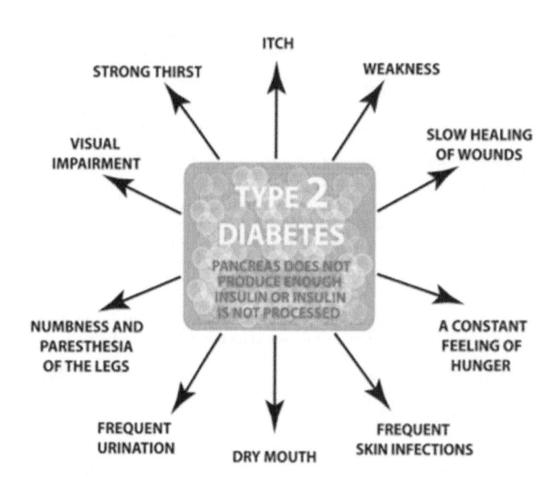

As type 2 diabetes progresses and becomes more serious, the symptoms can become highly uncomfortable and dangerous. Some of these advanced symptoms include:

- **Slow healing of bruises, cuts, and abrasions:** Many people suffering from type 2 diabetes have impaired immune systems due to the lack of energy available to the body. As well as a lack of energy, many diabetics have slowed circulation brought upon by high blood glucose levels. Both of these factors lead to a much slower healing process and far greater risks of infection.

- **Yeast infections:** Women with type 2 diabetes, the chances of yeast infections are far higher than in non-diabetic women. This is due to high blood sugar levels and a lowered immune system response.

- **Neuropathy or numbness:** Long-term high blood sugar levels can lead to severe nerve damage in adults with diabetes. It is believed around 70 percent of people with type 2 diabetes have some form of neuropathy (Hoskins, 2020). Diabetic neuropathy is characterized by a numbness in the extremities, specifically around the feet and fingers.

- **Dark skin patches (acanthosis nigricans):** Some people with type 2 diabetes may have far above normal levels of insulin in their blood, as their body is unable to utilize it due to insulin resistance. This rise of insulin in the bloodstream can lead to some skin cells over reproducing and cause black patches to form on the skin.

Complications

Severe complications of diabetes can be debilitating and deadly. Both type 1 & type 2 diabetes can cause serious neurological, cardiovascular, and optical conditions. Some of the most common complications of advanced diabetes are as follows:

- **Heart attacks:** Diabetes is directly linked to a higher rate of heart attacks in adults. High blood glucose levels damage the cells and nerves around the heart and blood vessels over time, which can cause a plethora of heart diseases to form.

- **Cataracts:** People with diabetes have a nearly 60 percent greater chance of developing cataracts later in life if their diabetes is left unchecked (Diabetes.co.uk, 2019a). Doctors are not sure of the real reason for cataracts forming at a higher rate in diabetes patients, but many believe it has to do with the lower amounts of glucose available to the cells powering our eyes.

- **Peripheral artery disease (PAD):** This is a very common diabetes and This causes decreased blood flow, which leads to serious issues in the lower legs, often resulting in amputation.

- **Diabetic nephropathy:** Diabetic nephropathy happens when high levels of blood glucose damage parts of your kidneys, which is responsible for filtering blood. This causes your kidneys to develop chronic kidney diseases and break down over time, leading to failure.

- **Glaucoma:** Diabetes can cause glaucoma in sufferers due to high blood sugar levels and this directly damages blood vessels in the eyes. When your body attempts to repair these vessels, it may cause glaucoma on the iris where the damage was caused.

10 Tips to Control Diabetes

- **Eat less salt:** Salt can increase your chances of having high blood pressure, which leads to increased chances of heart disease and stroke.

- **Replace sugar:** Replace sugar with zero calorie sweeteners. Cutting out sugar gives you much more control over your blood sugar levels.

- **Cut out alcohol:** Alcohol tends to be high in calories, and if drunk on an empty stomach with insulin medication, it can cause drastic drops in blood sugar.

- **Be physically active:** Physical action decreases your risk of cardiovascular issues and increases your body's natural glucose burn rate.

- **Avoid saturated fats:** Saturated fats like butter and pastries can lead to high cholesterol and blood circulation issues.

- **Use canola or olive oil:** If you need to use oil in your cooking, use canola or olive oil. Both are high in beneficial fatty acids and monounsaturated fat.

- **Drink water:** Water is by far the healthiest drink you can have. Drinking water helps to regulate blood sugar and insulin levels.

- **Make sure you get enough vitamin D:** Vitamin D is a crucial vitamin for controlling blood sugar levels. Eat food high in this vitamin or ask your doctor about supplements.

- **Avoid processed food:** Processed foods tend to be high in vegetable oils, salt, refined grains, or other unhealthy additives.

- **Drink coffee and tea:** Not only are coffee and tea great hunger suppressants for dieters, but they contain important antioxidants that help with protecting cells.

Type 1 vs Type 2 diabetes

Type 1 diabetes is an autoimmune disease. In cases of type 1 diabetes, the immune system attacks cells in the pancreas responsible for insulin production. Although we are unsure what causes this reaction, many experts believe it is brought upon by a gene deficiency or by viral infections that may trigger the disease.

Type 2 diabetes is a metabolic disorder, although research suggests it may warrant reclassification as an autoimmune disease as well. People who grieve from type 2 diabetes have a high resistance to insulin or an inability to produce enough insulin. Professionals believe that type 2 diabetes is a result of a genetic predisposition in many people, which is further aggravated by obesity and other environmental triggers.

Diagnosis

Diabetes diagnosis has come incredibly far in the last few decades. Currently, there are two primary tests for diagnosing diabetes: the fasting plasma glucose (FPG) test and the hemoglobin A1c test.

The FPG test takes your blood sugar levels after an eight-hour fasting period; this helps to show if your body is processing glucose at a healthy rate.

The A1c test shows your blood sugar levels over the last three months. It does this by testing the amount of glucose being carried by the hemoglobin of your red blood cells. Hemoglobin has a lifespan of roughly three months; this allows us to test them to see how long they have been carrying their glucose for and how much they have.

Chapter 1: How to Prevent Type 2 Diabetes

Diabetes mellitus is a disease that affects our metabolism. The predominant characteristic of diabetes is an inability to create or utilize insulin, a hormone that moves sugar from our blood cells into the rest of our bodies' cells. This is crucial for us because we rely on that blood sugar to power our body and provide energy. High blood sugar, if not treated, can lead to serious damage of our eyes, nerves, kidneys, and other major organs. There are 2 main types of diabetes, they are type 1 and type 2, with the second being the most common of the two with over 90 percent of diabetics suffering from it

Insulin resistance is the most popular cause of type 2 diabetes. Because muscle, fat, and liver cells no longer respond to insulin, the pancreas secretes a lot of it in order to keep blood sugar levels in check. Insulin resistance is exacerbated by being overweight and physically sedentary.

Prediabetes and glucose intolerance both cause insulin resistance. Prediabetes affects an estimated 79 million Americans. According to studies, decreasing 7% of your body weight and exercising regularly can reduce your risk of type 2 diabetes by 58 percent. Insulin resistance can be reduced by decreasing weight, exercising regularly, eating carbohydrates in moderation, and eating a nutritious diet once you've been diagnosed with diabetes. As a result, better blood sugar control will be achieved.

Type 2 diabetes is the most common form of the disease in adults. As we age, our cells don't use insulin as well and therefore cannot convert glucose into energy. The condition also increases your risk for serious health risks like heart disease, blindness, kidney failure, amputations and stroke.

The first step in preventing diabetes is to know what the risk factors are.

It all starts with your levels of glucose in the blood. This can be measured by two methods: fasting plasma glucose test and random plasma glucose test.

The number one cause of diabetes is family history: people who have a parent or sibling with type 1 or type 2 diabetes are likely to develop it themselves. If you want to lower your own risk, avoid early pregnancies, limit weight gain during pregnancy and breastfeed for at least two years. Also Know Your Glycemic Index To Help You Lose Weight.

The next step is to start eating right and exercising regularly.

• Eat a balanced diet. Include lean proteins (meat from chicken, fish or other lean sources). These foods provide building blocks for healthy muscles, skin and bones. Also eat a wide variety of foods. A varied diet provides the nutrients your body needs while preventing any known risk factors (such as heart disease) from occurring.

• Limit sugar to no more than 10% of your total daily calories. This limit means that you can eat foods like fruit, vegetables and other carbohydrates (like potatoes and pasta). You can also include some protein in your meals if these foods have little or no carbohydrate.

• Work out each day. The benefits are many: improved blood sugar control , weight-loss, increased energy and lower blood cholesterol levels .

• Reduce the amount of alcohol you drink . Drinking alcohol is a commonly implicated risk factor for diabetes. When alcohol is consumed, glucose levels go up because the liver must break down and store all the alcohol as fat. When this happens, insulin may be less effective at bringing glucose into the cells. This can lead to diabetes and heart disease over time.

• Take aspirin to reduce your risk of heart disease . The benefits are many: reduced blood cholesterol levels , less inflamed blood vessels , possibly fewer strokes , and even better memory . You should take a low-dose aspirin daily to reduce your risk of heart disease.

• Get regular exercise . Aerobic exercise like walking, swimming and dancing is beneficial for everyone but especially for people over 60 years old . There are many forms of aerobic exercises. Some are as simple as walking or stretching; others are more advanced. The American Diabetes Association suggests that you participate in an activity a minimum of 20 minutes three times per week (on nonconsecutive days).

• Get regular blood pressure checks .

• Stay away from tobacco . Smoking can lead to diabetes and is linked with a host of other diseases. Tobacco smoke contains more than 4,000 chemicals , many of which are known to damage a person's health. The nicotine in tobacco also gets into saliva and causes your body to absorb the more harmful chemicals even more rapidly. If you smoke, quit . The best way is to smoke a cigarette that contains only nicotine and no tobacco (such as an electronic cigarette) for a period of at least two weeks .

• Avoid heavy drinking . If you do drink alcohol, limit yourself to only one drink maximum per day (for women) or two drinks max per day (for guys).

• Learn your family history. If your family has diabetes, consult with a doctor who can help you lower your own risk by offering advice about food, physical activity and other factors that influence blood sugar levels and weight. If a parent or sibling has diabetes, it is important to talk with a doctor about whether genetic tests are recommended.

It is advisable to visit the doctor every 6 months for a check up and be aware of all the early symptoms of diabetes.

All in all, type 2 diabetes can be prevented by a balanced diet, regular exercise, weight loss and avoiding heavy drinking.

Chapter 2: Food to Eat

Vegetables

Fresh vegetables never cause harm to anyone. So, adding a meal full of vegetables is the best shot for all diabetic patients. But not all vegetables contain the same amount of macronutrients. Some vegetables contain a high amount of carbohydrates, so those are not suitable for a diabetic diet. We need to use vegetables which contain a low amount of carbohydrates.

1. Cauliflower

2. Spinach

3. Tomatoes

4. Broccoli

5. Lemons

6. Artichoke

7. Garlic

8. Asparagus

9. Spring onions

10. Onions

11. Ginger etc.

Meat

Meat is not on the red list for the diabetic diet. It is fine to have some meat every now and then for diabetic patients. However certain meat types are better than others. For instance, red meat is not a preferable option for such patients. They should consume white meat more often whether it's seafood or poultry. Healthy options in meat are:

1. All fish, i.e., salmon, halibut, trout, cod, sardine, etc.

2. Scallops

3. Mussels

4. Shrimp

5. Oysters etc.

Fruits

Not all fruits are good for diabetes. To know if the fruit is suitable for this diet, it is important to note its sugar content. Some fruits contain a high amount of sugars in the form of sucrose and fructose, and those should be readily avoided. Here is the list of popularly used fruits which can be taken on the diabetic diet:

1. Peaches

2. Nectarines

3. Avocados

4. Apples

5. Berries

6. Grapefruit

7. Kiwi Fruit

8. Bananas

9. Cherries

10. Grapes

11. Orange

12. Pears

13. Plums

14. Strawberries

Nuts and Seeds

Nuts and seeds are perhaps the most enriched edibles, and they contain such a mix of macronutrients which can never harm anyone. So diabetic patients can take the nuts and seeds in their diet without any fear of a glucose spike.

1. Pistachios

2. Sunflower seeds

3. Walnuts

4. Peanuts

5. Pecans

6. Pumpkin seeds

7. Almonds

8. Sesame seeds etc.

Grains

Diabetic patients should also be selective while choosing the right grains for their diet. The idea is to keep the amount of starch as minimum as possible. That is why you won't see any white rice in the list rather it is replaced with more fibrous brown rice.

1. Quinoa

2. Oats

3. Multigrain

4. Whole grains

5. Brown rice

6. Millet

7. Barley

8. Sorghum

9. Tapioca

Fats

Fat intake is the most debated topic as far as the diabetic diet is concerned. As there are diets like ketogenic, which are loaded with fats and still proved effective for diabetic patients. The key is the absence of carbohydrates. In any other situation, the fats are as harmful to diabetics as any normal person. Switching to unsaturated fats is a better option.

1. Sesame oil

2. Olive oil

3. Canola oil

4. Grapeseed oil

5. Other vegetable oils

6. Fats extracted from plant sources.

Diary

Any dairy product which directly or indirectly causes a glucose rise in the blood should not be taken on this diet. other than those, all products are good to use. These items include:

1. Skimmed milk

2. Low-fat cheese

3. Eggs

4. Yogurt

5. Trans fat-free margarine or butter

Sugar Alternatives

Since ordinary sugars or sweeteners are strictly forbidden on a diabetic diet. There are artificial varieties that can add sweetness without raising the level of carbohydrates in the meal. These substitutes are:

1. Stevia

2. Xylitol

3. Natvia

4. Swerve

5. Monk fruit

6. Erythritol

Make sure to substitute them with extra care. The sweetness of each sweetener is entirely different from the table sugar, so add each in accordance with the intensity of their flavor. Stevia is the sweetest of them, and it should be used with more care. In place of 1 cup of sugar, a teaspoon of stevia is enough. All other sweeteners are more or less similar to sugar in their intensity of sweetness.

Foods to Avoid

Knowing a general scheme of diet helps a lot, but it is equally important to be well familiar with the items which have to be avoided. With this list, you can make your diet a hundred% sugar-free. There are many other food items which can cause some harm to a diabetic patient as the sugars do. So, let's discuss them in some detail here.

1. Sugars

Sugar is a big NO-GO for a diabetic diet. Once you are diabetic, you would need to say goodbye to all the natural sweeteners which are loaded with carbohydrates. They contain polysaccharides which readily break into glucose after getting into our body. And the list does not only include table sugars but other items like honey and molasses should also be avoided.

1. White sugar

2. Brown sugar

3. Confectionary sugar

4. Honey

5. Molasses

6. Granulated sugar

Your mind and your body, will not accept the abrupt change. It is recommended to go for a gradual change. It means start substituting it with low carb substitutes in a small amount, day by day.

2. High Fat Dairy Products

Once you are diabetic, you may get susceptible to a number of other fatal diseases including cardiovascular ones. That is why experts strictly recommend avoiding high-fat food products, especially dairy items. The high amount of fat can make your body insulin resistant. So even when you take insulin, it won't be of any use as the body will not work on it.

3. Saturated Animal Fats

Saturated animal fats are not good for anyone, whether diabetic or normal. So, better avoid using them in general. Whenever you are cooking meat, try to trim off all the excess fat. Cooking oils made out of these saturated fats should be avoided. Keep yourself away from any of the animal origin fats.

4. High Carb Vegetables

As discussed above, vegetables with more starch are not suitable for diabetes. These veggies can increase the carbohydrate levels of food. So, omit these from the recipes and enjoy the rest of the less starchy vegetables. Some of the high carb vegetables are:

1. Potatoes

2. Sweet potatoes

3. Yams etc.

5. Cholesterol Rich ingredients

Bad cholesterol or High-density Lipoprotein has the tendency to deposit in different parts of the body. That is why food items having high bad cholesterol are not good for diabetes. Such items should be replaced with the ones with low cholesterol.

6. High Sodium Products

Sodium is related to hypertension and blood pressure. Since diabetes is already the result of a hormonal imbalance in the body, in the presence of excess sodium — another imbalance — a fluid imbalance may occur which a diabetic body cannot tolerate. It adds up to already present complications of the disease. So, avoid using food items with a high amount of sodium. Mainly store packed items, processed foods, and salt all contain sodium, and one should avoid them all. Use only the 'Unsalted' variety of food products, whether it's butter, margarine, nuts, or other items.

7. Sugary Drinks

Cola drinks or other similar beverages are filled with sugars. If you had seen different video presentations showing the amount of the sugars present in a single bottle of soda, you would know how dangerous those are for diabetic patients. They can drastically increase the amount of blood glucose level within 30 minutes of drinking. Fortunately, there are many sugar-free varieties available in the drinks which are suitable for diabetic patients.

8. Sugar Syrups and Toppings

A number of syrups available in the markets are made out of nothing but sugar. Maple syrup is one good example. For a diabetic diet, the patient should avoid such sugary syrups and also stay away from the sugar-rich toppings available in the stores. If you want to use them at all, trust yourself and prepare them at home with a sugar-free recipe.

9. Sweet Chocolate and candies

For diabetic patients, sugar-free chocolates or candies are the best way out. Other processed chocolate bars and candies are extremely damaging to their health, and all of these should be avoided. You can try and prepare healthy bars and candies at home with sugar-free recipes.

10. Alcohol

Alcohol has the tendency to reduce the rate of our metabolism and take away our appetite, which can render a diabetic patient into a very life-threatening condition. Alcohol in a very small amount cannot harm the patient, but the regular or constant intake of alcohol is bad for health and glucose levels.

The importance of insuline

Diabetes is a serious condition caused by a deficiency of insulin. Insulin is a hormone that is necessary for the proper functioning of the body. When a person develops diabetes, the cells in the body do not respond to insulin properly. The result is that the cells do not get the energy and nutrients they need, and then they start to die

Diabetes treatments differ depending on the kind, number, and severity of complications as well as the patient's overall health. Fortunately, diabetes has been studied extensively by the medical community, and as a result, there are numerous resources and treatments accessible.

For type 1 diabetes, insulin supplements are essential. Type 1 diabetics rely on daily insulin injections; some prefer a costlier but easier-to-use insulin pump. Insulin needs in type 1 diabetics will vary throughout the day as they eat and exercise. This means many type 1 diabetics will regularly test their blood sugar levels to assess whether their insulin needs are being met.

Some type 1 diabetics develop insulin resistance after years of injections. This means that oral diabetes medication such as metformin is becoming increasingly more commonly prescribed to type 1 diabetics to help prevent insulin resistance.

In some circumstances, type 2 diabetes can be managed without the need of medication. Many type 2 diabetics individuals can control their blood sugar levels by watching what they eat and doing some modest exercise. The majority of type 2 diabetics are advised to stick to low-fat, high-fiber, low-carbohydrate diets.

Medication is required for some persons with type 2 diabetes. Type 2 diabetes, unlike type 1, does not demand the use of insulin as frequently. Some type 2 diabetics, however, require insulin to complement their pancreas' production.

Metformin is the most widely given type 2 diabetic medication. This prescription medication aids in the reduction of blood glucose levels and the improvement of insulin sensitivity. Other drugs prescribed to type 2 diabetics include sulfonylureas, thiazolidinediones, and meglitinides, which all help increase insulin production or sensitivity.

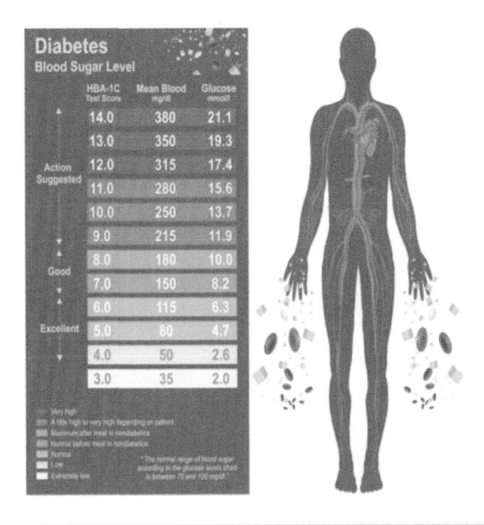

Causes of Type 2 diabetes

Although some of the causes are completely unclear, even trivial viral infections are recognized, which can affect insulin-producing cells in the pancreas, such as:

- Measles.

- Cytomegalovirus.

- Epstein-Barr.

- Coxsackievirus.

For Type 2 Diabetes, however, the main risk factors are:

- Overweight and obesity.

- Genetic factors: family history increases the risk of developing type 2 diabetes.

21

- Ethnicity: the highest number of cases is recorded in the populations of sub-Saharan Africa and the middle east and north Africa.

- Environmental factors are especially related to incorrect lifestyles (sedentary lifestyle and obesity).

- Gestational diabetes, which is diabetes that happens during pregnancy.

- Age: type 2 diabetes increases with increasing age, especially above the age of 65.

- Diet high in fat that promotes obesity.

- Alcohol consumption.

- Sedentary lifestyle.

Chapter 3: Antidiabetic Life-Style, Develop Good Habits

We all know that healthy living is key to living well and feeling better. When it comes to diabetes, a healthy lifestyle can help control the condition and make it more manageable. What's an anti-diabetic lifestyle? It's all the things we need to do on a daily basis to keep ourselves in good health, including eating right, getting plenty of exercise, staying at a healthy weight and going easy on stress.

Diabetes is a chronic disorder of the endocrine system that occurs over time when your body cannot produce or respond to insulin. This can lead to excessive blood glucose levels.

The American Diabetes Association estimates that around 29 million Americans have diabetes, which translates into 9% of the population having diabetes.

One of the symptoms of diabetes is high blood glucose levels. This is why people with diabetes need to regularly monitor their blood glucose levels and have a healthy diet, with regular exercise.

Your doctor will recommend that you follow an antidiabetic lifestyle. It will give you stable blood glucose levels, which means fewer or no possible complications.

An anti-diabetic lifestyle consists of 4 parts: healthy food habits, physical activity pattern , monitoring blood glucose levels and self care . Following this lifestyle can help to prevent weight gain and reduce your risk for further complications from diabetes. It can also help to improve your overall health and help you live longer.

If you already have diabetes, an anti-diabetic lifestyle can help manage your blood glucose levels and prevent or delay complications. It is a healthy choice for all people with diabetes, regardless of the type.

In order to maintain this healthy lifestyle and achieve stable blood glucose levels, you will need to manage your weight, avoid unhealthy habits like smoking and alcohol abuse and follow the medical advice given by your doctor.

The following tips will prepare you for an anti-diabetic lifestyle:

Choose healthy food:

Eat a variety of foods like fruits, vegetables, whole grains, legumes and nuts that are rich in fiber.

Avoid junk food :

Choose healthy snacks and drinks like vegetables, fruits and milk.

Eat breakfast :

Breakfast is very important to stay healthy. Eat 'real' foods as often as you can . A small amount of protein at each meal has been shown to reduce the risk of heart disease in people with diabetes. Get most of your calories from carbohydrate foods (e.g., whole grain breads, cereals, pasta, potatoes) rather than fat or cholesterol-rich foods (e.g., ice cream).

Avoid excess fat:

Try to take the first meal of the day with a carbohydrate-rich food and avoid eating large amounts of fat and protein.

Avoid alcohol consumption:

If you drink alcohol, try to have it in moderation . Avoid excessive consumption of alcohol. Drinking too much can raise your blood glucose levels.

Monitor your weight:

If you are overweight, lose some weight to improve your health and lower your blood sugar. If you are underweight, try to gain some weight to reduce risk for complications from diabetes.

So all it takes is living in a more natural and efficient way and you will reduce your chances of getting sick or becoming chronically ill. In fact, there are many other studies that prove not only that yoga can help cure chronic illnesses but it can also prevent them from happening in the first place. A recent study conducted by the University of Kansas looked at the untapped benefits of yoga, and found that it has 'miraculous' effects on reducing stress and disease. They added: 'Yoga is a therapeutic style that combines physical postures, controlled breathing techniques, meditation and contemplation. It is often thought to be an ancient Indian practice, but it has been included in the revised American Heritage Dictionary since the 1970s.' The NIH (National Institute of Health) and VA (Veterans Administration) have collaborated to create a series of health care resources for veterans called Warrior Yoga™. These resources are intended to help veterans manage their stress through yoga, and are credited for helping decrease instances of PTSD (Post Traumatic Stress Disorder) by 40% in the first year of participation.

Chapter 4: Appendix Measurements Conversion

GAS MARK	DEGREE CELCIUS °C	DEGREE CELSIUS FAN °C	DEGREE FAHRENHEIT °F
1/4	110°C	100°C	225 °F
1/2	120°C	110°C	250 °F
1	140°C	120°C	275 °F
2	150°C	130°C	300 °F
3	170°C	140°C	325 °F
4	180°C	160°C	350 °F
5	190 °C	170°C	375 °F
6	200 °C	180°C	400 °F
7	220 °C	200°C	425 °F
8	230 °C	210°C	450 °F
9	240 °C	220°C	475 °F
10	260 °C	240°C	500 °F

Volume Conversions		
Metric	**Imperial**	**US Cups**
250ml	8 fl oz	1 cup
180ml	6 fl oz	¾ cup
150 ml	5fl oz	⅔ cup
120ml	4 fl oz	½ cup
75ml	2 ½ fl oz	⅓ cup
60ml	2 fl oz	¼ cup
30 ml	1 fl oz	⅛ cup
15ml	½ fl oz	1 tablespoon

Grams	Pounds & Ounces
10 g	0.25 oz
20 g	0.75 oz
25 g	1 oz
40 g	1.50 oz
50 g	2 oz
60 g	2.5 oz
75 g	3 oz
110 g	4 oz
125 g	4.5 oz
150 g	5 oz
175 g	6 oz
200 g	7 oz
225 g	8 oz
250 g	9 oz
350 g	12 oz
450 g	1 lb
700 g	1 lb 8oz
900 g	2 lb
1.35 kg	3lb

Chapter 5: Recipes

Breakfast Recipes

1. Bacon and Chicken Garlic Wrap

Preparation Time: 15 minutes

Cooking Time: 10 minutes

Servings: 4

Ingredients

- 1 chicken fillet, cut into small cubes

- 8-9 thin slices bacon, cut to fit cubes

- 6 garlic cloves, minced

Directions:

1. Preheat your oven to 400 degrees F

2. Line a baking tray with aluminum foil

3. Add minced garlic to a bowl and rub each chicken piece with it

4. Wrap bacon piece around each garlic chicken bite

5. Secure with toothpick

6. Transfer bites to the baking sheet, keeping a little bit of space between them

7. Bake for about 15-20 minutes until crispy

8. Serve and enjoy!

Nutrition: Calories: 260 Fat: 19g Carbs: 5g Protein: 22g Sugar: 12g; Fiber: 3g; Sodium: 187mg

2. Salty Macadamia Smoothie

Preparation Time: 5 minutes

Cooking Time: Nil

Servings: 1

Ingredients

- 2 tablespoons macadamia nuts, salted

- 1/3 cup chocolate whey protein powder, low carb

- 1 cup almond milk, unsweetened

Directions:

1. Add the listed ingredients to your blender and blend until you have a smooth mixture

2. Chill and enjoy it!

Nutrition: Calories: 165 Fat: 2g Carbs: 1g Protein: 12g Sugar: 8 g; Fiber: 4g; Sodium: 192mg

3. Buckwheat grouts breakfast bowl

Preparation time: 5 minutes, plus overnight to soak

Cooking time: 10 to 12 minutes

Servings: 4

Ingredients:

- 3 cups skim milk

- 1 cup buckwheat grouts

- ¼ cup chia seeds

- 2 teaspoons vanilla extract

- 1/2 teaspoon ground cinnamon

- Pinch salt

- 1 cup water

- 1/2 cup unsalted pistachios

- 2 cups sliced fresh strawberries

- ¼ cup cacao nibs (optional)

Directions:

1. In a large bowl, stir together the milk, groats, chia seeds, vanilla, cinnamon, and salt. Cover and refrigerate overnight.

2. The next morning, transfer the soaked mixture to a medium pot and add the water. Bring to a boil over medium-high heat, reduce the heat to maintain a simmer, and cook for 10 to 12 minutes, until the buckwheat is tender and thickened.

3. Transfer to bowls and serve, topped with the pistachios, strawberries, and cacao nibs (if using).

Nutrition: Calories: 340; Fat: 8g; Carbs: 52g; Protein: 15g; Sugar: 14g; Fiber: 10g; Sodium: 140mg

4. Peach muesli bake

Preparation time: 10 minutes

Cooking time: 40 minutes

Servings: 4

Ingredients:

- Nonstick cooking spray

- 2 cups skim milk

- 11/2 cups rolled oats

- 1/2 cup chopped walnuts

- 1 large egg

- 2 tablespoons maple syrup

- 1 teaspoon ground cinnamon

- 1 teaspoon baking powder

- 1/2 teaspoon salt

- 2 to 3 peaches, sliced

Directions:

1. Preheat the oven to 375f. Spray a 9-inch square baking dish with cooking spray. Set aside.

2. In a large bowl, stir together the milk, oats, walnuts, egg, maple syrup, cinnamon, baking powder, and salt. Spread half the mixture in the prepared baking dish.

3. Place half the peaches in a single layer across the oat mixture.

4. Spread the remaining oat mixture over the top. Add the remaining peaches in a thin layer over the oats. Bake for 35 to 40 minutes, uncovered, until thickened and browned.

5. Cut into 8 squares and serve warm.

Nutrition: Calories: 138; Fat: 3g; Protein: 6g; Carbs: 22g; Sugar: 10g; Fiber: 3g; Sodium: 191mg

5. Steel-cut oatmeal bowl with fruit and nuts

Preparation time: 5 minutes

Cooking time: 20 minutes

Servings: 4

Ingredients:

- 1 cup steel-cut oats

- 2 cups almond milk

- ¾ cup water

- 1 teaspoon ground cinnamon

- ¼ teaspoon salt

- 2 cups chopped fresh fruit, such as blueberries, strawberries, raspberries, or peaches

- 1/2 cup chopped walnuts

- ¼ cup chia seeds

Directions:

1. In a medium saucepan over medium-high heat, combine the oats, almond milk, water, cinnamon, and salt. Bring to a boil, reduce the heat to low, and simmer for 15 to 20 minutes, until the oats are softened and thickened.

2. Top each bowl with 1/2 cup of fresh fruit, 2 tablespoons of walnuts, and 1 tablespoon of chia seeds before serving.

Nutrition: Calories: 288; Fat: 11g; Protein: 10g; Carbs: 38g; Sugar: 7g; Fiber: 10g; Sodium: 329mg

6. Whole-grain dutch baby pancake

Preparation time: 5 minutes

Cooking time: 25 minutes

Servings: 4

Ingredients:

- 2 tablespoons coconut oil

- 1/2 cup whole-wheat flour

- ¼ cup skim milk

- 3 large eggs

- 1 teaspoon vanilla extract

- 1/2 teaspoon baking powder

- ¼ teaspoon salt

- ¼ teaspoon ground cinnamon

- Powdered sugar, for dusting

Directions:

1. Preheat the oven to 400f.

2. Put the coconut oil in a medium oven-safe skillet, and place the skillet in the oven to melt the oil while it preheats.

3. In a blender, combine the flour, milk, eggs, vanilla, baking powder, salt, and cinnamon. Process until smooth.

4. Carefully remove the skillet from the oven and tilt to spread the oil around evenly.

5. Pour the batter into the skillet and return it to the oven for 23 to 25 minutes, until the pancake puffs and lightly browns.

6. Remove, dust lightly with powdered sugar, cut into 4 wedges, and serve.

Nutrition: Calories: 195; Fat: 11g; Protein: 8g; Carbs: 16g; Sugar: 1g; Fiber: 2g; Sodium: 209mg

7. Mushroom, zucchini, and onion frittata

Preparation time: 10 minutes

Cooking time: 20 minutes

Servings: 4

Ingredients:

- 1 tablespoon extra-virgin olive oil

- 1/2 onion, chopped

- 1 medium zucchini, chopped

- 11/2 cups sliced mushrooms

- 6 large eggs, beaten

- 2 tablespoons skim milk

- Salt

- Freshly ground black pepper

- 1 ounce feta cheese, crumbled

Directions:

1. Preheat the oven to 400f.

2. In a medium oven-safe skillet over medium-high heat, heat the olive oil.

3. Add the onion and sauté for 3 to 5 minutes, until translucent.

4. Add the zucchini and mushrooms, and cook for 3 to 5 more minutes, until the vegetables are tender.

5. Meanwhile, in a small bowl, whisk the eggs, milk, salt, and pepper. Pour the mixture into the skillet, stirring to combine, and transfer the skillet to the oven. Cook for 7 to 9 minutes, until set.

6. Sprinkle with the feta cheese, and cook for 1 to 2 minutes more, until heated through.

7. Remove, cut into 4 wedges, and serve.

Nutrition: Calories: 178; Fat: 13g; Protein: 12g; Carbs: 5g; Sugar: 3g; Fiber: 1g; Sodium: 234mg

8.   Berry-oat breakfast bars

Preparation time: 10 minutes

Cooking time: 25 minutes

Servings: 2

Ingredients:

- 2 cups fresh raspberries or blueberries

- 2 tablespoons sugar

- 2 tablespoons freshly squeezed lemon juice

- 1 tablespoon cornstarch

- 11/2 cups rolled oats

- 1/2 cup whole-wheat flour

- 1/2 cup walnuts

- ¼ cup chia seeds

- ¼ cup extra-virgin olive oil

- ¼ cup honey

- 1 large egg

Directions:

1. Preheat the oven to 350f.

2. In a small saucepan over medium heat, stir together the berries, sugar, lemon juice, and cornstarch. Bring to a simmer. Reduce the heat and simmer for 2 to 3 minutes, until the mixture thickens.

3. In a food processor or high-speed blender, combine the oats, flour, walnuts, and chia seeds. Process until powdered. Add the olive oil, honey, and egg. Pulse a few more times, until well combined. Press half of the mixture into a 9-inch square baking dish.

4. Spread the berry filling over the oat mixture. Add the remaining oat mixture on top of the berries. Bake for 25 minutes, until browned.

5. Let cool completely, cut into 12 pieces, and serve. Store in a covered container for up to 5 days.

Nutrition: Calories: 201; Fat: 10g; Protein: 5g; Carbs: 26g; Sugar: 9g; Fiber: 5g; Sodium: 8mg

9. Spinach and cheese quiche

Preparation time: 10 minutes, plus 10 minutes to rest

Cooking time: 50 minutes

Servings: 4

Ingredients:

- Nonstick cooking spray
- 8 ounces yukon gold potatoes, shredded
- 1 tablespoon plus 2 teaspoons extra-virgin olive oil, divided
- 1 teaspoon salt, divided
- Freshly ground black pepper
- 1 onion, finely chopped
- 1 (10-ounce) bag fresh spinach
- 4 large eggs
- 1/2 cup skim milk
- 1 ounce gruyère cheese, shredded

Directions:

1. Preheat the oven to 350f. Spray a 9-inch pie dish with cooking spray. Set aside.

2. In a small bowl, toss the potatoes with 2 teaspoons of olive oil, 1/2 teaspoon of salt, and season with pepper. Press the potatoes into the bottom and sides of the pie dish to form a thin, even layer. Bake for 20 minutes, until golden brown. Remove from the oven and set aside to cool.

3. In a large skillet over medium-high heat, heat the remaining 1 tablespoon of olive oil.

4. Add the onion and sauté for 3 to 5 minutes, until softened.

5. By handfuls, add the spinach, stirring between each addition, until it just starts to wilt before adding more. Cook for about 1 minute, until it cooks down.

6. In a medium bowl, whisk the eggs and milk. Add the gruyère, and season with the remaining 1/2 teaspoon of salt and some pepper. Fold the eggs into the spinach. Pour the mixture into the pie dish and bake for 25 minutes, until the eggs are set.

7. Let rest for 10 minutes before serving.

Nutrition: Calories: 445; Fat: 14g; Protein: 19g; Carbs: 68g; Sugar: 6g; Fiber: 7g; Sodium: 773mg

10. Spicy Jalapeno Popper Deviled Eggs

Preparation Time: 5 minutes

Cooking Time: 5 minutes

Servings: 4

Ingredients

- 4 large whole eggs, hardboiled
- 2 tablespoons Keto-Friendly mayonnaise
- ¼ cup cheddar cheese, grated
- 2 slices bacon, cooked and crumbled
- 1 jalapeno, sliced

Directions:

1. Cut eggs in half, remove the yolk and put them in bowl

2. Lay egg whites on a platter

3. Mix in remaining ingredients and mash them with the egg yolks

4. Transfer yolk mix back to the egg whites

5. Serve and enjoy!

Nutrition: Calories: 176 Fat: 14g Carbs: 0.7g Protein: 10g Sugar: 10g; Fiber: 7g; Sodium: 653mg

11. Blueberry breakfast cake

Preparation time: 15 minutes

Cooking time: 45 minutes

Servings: 4

Ingredients:

For the topping

- ¼ cup finely chopped walnuts

- 1/2 teaspoon ground cinnamon

- 2 tablespoons butter, chopped into small pieces

- 2 tablespoons sugar

For the cake

- Nonstick cooking spray

- 1 cup whole-wheat pastry flour

- 1 cup oat flour

- ¼ cup sugar

- 2 teaspoons baking powder

- 1 large egg, beaten

- 1/2 cup skim milk

- 2 tablespoons butter, melted

- 1 teaspoon grated lemon peel

- 2 cups fresh or frozen blueberries

Directions:

To make the topping

In a small bowl, stir together the walnuts, cinnamon, butter, and sugar. Set aside.

To make the cake

1. Preheat the oven to 350f. Spray a 9-inch square pan with cooking spray. Set aside.

2. In a large bowl, stir together the pastry flour, oat flour, sugar, and baking powder.

3. Add the egg, milk, butter, and lemon peel, and stir until there are no dry spots.

4. Stir in the blueberries, and gently mix until incorporated. Press the batter into the prepared pan, using a spoon to flatten it into the dish.

5. Sprinkle the topping over the cake.

6. Bake for 40 to 45 minutes, until a toothpick inserted into the cake comes out clean, and serve.

Nutrition: Calories: 177; Fat: 7g; Protein: 4g; Carbs: 26g; Sugar: 9g; Fiber: 3g; Sodium: 39mg

12. Lovely Porridge

Preparation Time: 15 minutes

Cooking Time: Nil

Servings: 2

Ingredients

- 2 tablespoons coconut flour

- 2 tablespoons vanilla protein powder

- 3 tablespoons Golden Flaxseed meal

- 1 and 1/2 cups almond milk, unsweetened

- Powdered erythritol

Directions:

1. Take a bowl and mix in flaxseed meal, protein powder, coconut flour and mix well

2. Add mix to the saucepan (placed over medium heat)

3. Add almond milk and stir, let the mixture thicken

4. Add your desired amount of sweetener and serve

5. Enjoy!

Nutrition: Calories: 259 Fat: 13g Carbs: 5g Protein: 16g Sugar: 14g; Fiber: 10g; Sodium: 140mg

13. Basil and Tomato Baked Eggs

Preparation Time: 10 minutes

Cooking Time: 15 minutes

Servings: 4

Ingredients

- 1 garlic clove, minced

- 1 cup canned tomatoes

- ¼ cup fresh basil leaves, roughly chopped

- 1/2 teaspoon chili powder

- 1 tablespoon olive oil

- 4 whole eggs

- Salt and pepper to taste

Directions:

1. Preheat your oven to 375 degrees F

2. Take a small baking dish and grease with olive oil

3. Add garlic, basil, tomatoes chili, olive oil into a dish and stir

4. Crackdown eggs into a dish, keeping space between the two

5. Sprinkle the whole dish with salt and pepper

6. Place in oven and cook for 12 minutes until eggs are set and tomatoes are bubbling

7. Serve with basil on top

8. Enjoy!

Nutrition: Calories: 235 Fat: 16g Carbs: 7g Protein: 14g Sugar: 18g; Fiber: 13g; Sodium: 142mg

14. Whole-grain pancakes

Preparation time: 10 minutes

Cooking time: 15 minutes

Servings: 4

Ingredients:

- 2 cups whole-wheat pastry flour

- 4 teaspoons baking powder

- 2 teaspoons ground cinnamon

- 1/2 teaspoon salt

- 2 cups skim milk, plus more as needed

- 2 large eggs

- 1 tablespoon honey

- Nonstick cooking spray

- Maple syrup, for serving

- Fresh fruit, for serving

Directions:

1. In a large bowl, stir together the flour, baking powder, cinnamon, and salt.

2. Add the milk, eggs, and honey, and stir well to combine. If needed, add more milk, 1 tablespoon at a time, until there are no dry spots and you has a pourable batter.

3. Heat a large skillet over medium-high heat, and spray it with cooking spray.

4. Using a ¼-cup measuring cup, scoop 2 or 3 pancakes into the skillet at a time. Cook for a couple of minutes, until bubbles form on the surface of the pancakes, flip, and cook for 1 to 2 minutes more, until golden brown and cooked through. Repeat with the remaining batter.

5. Serve topped with maple syrup or fresh fruit.

Nutrition: Calories: 392; Fat: 4g; Protein: 15g; Carbs: 71g; Sugar: 11g; Fiber: 9g; Sodium: 396mg

15.   Whole-grain breakfast cookies

Preparation time: 20 minutes

Cooking time: 10 minutes

Servings: 18 cookies

Ingredients:

- 2 cups rolled oats

- 1/2 cup whole-wheat flour

- ¼ cup ground flaxseed

- 1 teaspoon baking powder

- 1 cup unsweetened applesauce

- 2 large eggs

- 2 tablespoons vegetable oil

- 2 teaspoons vanilla extract

- 1 teaspoon ground cinnamon

- 1/2 cup dried cherries

- ¼ cup unsweetened shredded coconut

- 2 ounces dark chocolate, chopped

Directions:

1. Preheat the oven to 350f.

2. In a large bowl, combine the oats, flour, flaxseed, and baking powder. Stir well to mix.

3. In a medium bowl, whisk the applesauce, eggs, vegetable oil, vanilla, and cinnamon. Pour the wet mixture into the dry mixture, and stir until just combined.

4. Fold in the cherries, coconut, and chocolate. Drop tablespoon-size balls of dough onto a baking sheet. Bake for 10 to 12 minutes, until browned and cooked through.

5. Let cool for about 3 minutes, remove from the baking sheet, and cool completely before serving. Store in an airtight container for up to 1 week.

Nutrition: Calories: 136; Fat: 7g; Protein: 4g; Carbs: 14g; Sugar: 4g; Fiber: 3g; Sodium: 11mg

16.   Cinnamon and Coconut Porridge

Preparation Time: 5 minutes

Cooking Time: 5 minutes

Servings: 4

Ingredients

- 2 cups of water

- 1 cup 36% heavy cream
- 1/2 cup unsweetened dried coconut, shredded
- 2 tablespoons flaxseed meal
- 1 tablespoon butter
- 1 and 1/2 teaspoon stevia
- 1 teaspoon cinnamon
- Salt to taste
- Toppings as blueberries

Directions:

1. Add the listed ingredients to a small pot, mix well
2. Transfer pot to stove and place it over medium-low heat
3. Bring to mix to a slow boil
4. Stir well and remove the heat
5. Divide the mix into equal servings and let them sit for 10 minutes
6. Top with your desired toppings and enjoy!

Nutrition: Calories: 171 Fat: 16g Carbs: 6g Protein: 2g Sugar: 14g; Fiber: 10g; Sodium: 140mg

17. An Omelet of Swiss chard

Preparation Time: 5 minutes

Cooking Time: 5 minutes

Servings: 4

Ingredients

- 4 eggs, lightly beaten
- 4 cups Swiss chard, sliced
- 2 tablespoons butter
- 1/2 teaspoon garlic salt
- Fresh pepper

Directions:

1. Take a non-stick frying pan and place it over medium-low heat
2. Once the butter melts, add Swiss chard and stir cook for 2 minutes
3. Pour egg into the pan and gently stir them into Swiss chard
4. Season with garlic salt and pepper
5. Cook for 2 minutes
6. Serve and enjoy!

Nutrition: Calories: 260 Fat: 21g Carbs: 4g Protein: 14g Sugar: 12g; Fiber: 8g; Sodium: 137mg

18. Cheesy Low-Carb Omelet

Preparation Time: 5 minutes

Cooking Time: 5 minutes

Servings: 3

Ingredients

- 2 whole eggs
- 1 tablespoon water
- 1 tablespoon butter
- 3 thin slices salami
- 5 fresh basil leaves
- 5 thin slices, fresh ripe tomatoes

- 2 ounces fresh mozzarella cheese

- Salt and pepper as needed

Directions:

1. Take a small bowl and whisk in eggs and water

2. Take a non-stick Sauté pan and place it over medium heat, add butter and let it melt

3. Pour egg mixture and cook for 30 seconds

4. Spread salami slices on half of egg mix and top with cheese, tomatoes, basil slices

5. Season with salt and pepper according to your taste

6. Cook for 2 minutes and fold the egg with the empty half

7. Cover and cook on LOW for 1 minute

8. Serve and enjoy!

Nutrition: Calories: 451 Fat: 36g Carbs: 3g Protein:33g Sugar: 11g; Fiber: 14g; Sodium: 134mg

19. Yogurt and Kale Smoothie

Preparation Time: 10 minutes

Servings: 1

Ingredients:

- 1 cup whole milk yogurt

- 1 cup baby kale greens

- 1 pack stevia

- 1 tablespoon MCT oil

- 1 tablespoon sunflower seeds

- 1 cup of water

Directions:

1. Add listed ingredients to the blender

2. Blend until you have a smooth and creamy texture

3. Serve chilled and enjoy!

Nutrition: Calories: 329 Fat: 26g Carbs: 15g Protein: 11g Sugar: 10g; Fiber: 15g; Sodium: 144mg

20. Grilled Chicken Platter

Preparation Time: 5 minutes

Cooking Time: 10 minutes

Servings: 3

Ingredients

- 3 large chicken breast, sliced half lengthwise

- 10-ounce spinach, frozen and drained

- 3-ounce mozzarella cheese, part-skim

- 1/2 a cup of roasted red peppers, cut in long strips

- 1 teaspoon of olive oil

- 2 garlic cloves, minced

- Salt and pepper as needed

Directions:

1. Preheat your oven to 400 degrees Fahrenheit

2. Slice 3 chicken breast lengthwise

3. Take a non-stick pan and grease with cooking spray

4. Bake for 2-3 minutes each side

5. Take another skillet and cook spinach and garlic in oil for 3 minutes

6. Place chicken on an oven pan and top with spinach, roasted peppers, and mozzarella

7. Bake until the cheese melted

8. Enjoy!

Nutrition: Calories: 195 Fat: 7g Protein: 30g Sugar: 14g; Fiber: 10g; Sodium: 140mg

21.   Parsley Chicken Breast

Preparation Time: 10 minutes

Cooking Time: 40 minutes

Servings: 4

Ingredients

- 1 tablespoon dry parsley

- 1 tablespoon dry basil

- 4 chicken breast halves, boneless and skinless

- 1/2 teaspoon salt

- 1/2 teaspoon red pepper flakes, crushed

- 2 tomatoes, sliced

Directions:

1. Preheat your oven to 350 degrees F

2. Take a 9x13 inch baking dish and grease it up with cooking spray

3. Sprinkle 1 tablespoon of parsley, 1 teaspoon of basil and spread the mixture over your baking dish

4. Arrange the chicken breast halves over the dish and sprinkle garlic slices on top

5. Take a small bowl and add 1 teaspoon parsley, 1 teaspoon of basil, salt, basil, red pepper and mix well. Pour the mixture over the chicken breast

6. Top with tomato slices and cover, bake for 25 minutes

7. Remove the cover and bake for 15 minutes more

8. Serve and enjoy!

Nutrition: Calories: 150 Fat: 4g Carbs: 4g Protein: 25g Sugar: 17g; Fiber: 7g; Sodium: 133mg

22.   Mustard Chicken

Preparation Time: 10 minutes

Cooking Time: 40 minutes

Servings: 2

Ingredients

- 4 chicken breasts

- 1/2 cup chicken broth

- 3-4 tablespoons mustard

- 3 tablespoons olive oil

- 1 teaspoon paprika

- 1 teaspoon chili powder

- 1 teaspoon garlic powder

Directions:

1. Take a small bowl and mix mustard, olive oil, paprika, chicken broth, garlic powder, chicken broth, and chili

2. Add chicken breast and marinate for 30 minutes

3. Take a lined baking sheet and arrange the chicken

4. Bake for 35 minutes at 375 degrees Fahrenheit

5. Serve and enjoy!

Nutrition: Calories: 531 Fat: 23g Carbs: 10g Protein: 64g Sugar: 14g; Fiber: 12g; Sodium: 148mg

23. Balsamic Chicken

Preparation Time: 10 minutes

Cooking Time: 25 minutes

Servings: 3

Ingredients

- 6 chicken breast halves, skinless and boneless

- 1 teaspoon garlic salt

- Ground black pepper

- 2 tablespoons olive oil

- 1 onion, thinly sliced

- 14 and 1/2 ounces tomatoes, diced

- 1/2 cup balsamic vinegar

- 1 teaspoon dried basil

- 1 teaspoon dried oregano

- 1 teaspoon dried rosemary

- 1/2 teaspoon dried thyme

Directions:

1. Season both sides of your chicken breasts thoroughly with pepper and garlic salt

2. Take a skillet and place it over medium heat

3. Add some oil and cook your seasoned chicken for 3-4 minutes per side until the breasts are nicely browned

4. Add some onion and cook for another 3-4 minutes until the onions are browned

5. Pour the diced up tomatoes and balsamic vinegar over your chicken and season with some rosemary, basil, thyme, and rosemary

6. Simmer the chicken for about 15 minutes until they are no longer pink

7. Take an instant-read thermometer and check if the internal temperature gives a reading of 165 degrees Fahrenheit

8. If yes, then you are good to go!

Nutrition: Calories: 196 Fat: 7g Carbs: 7g Protein: 23g Sugar: 10g; Fiber: 12g; Sodium: 142mg

24. Greek Chicken Breast

Preparation Time: 10 minutes

Cooking Time: 25 minutes

Servings: 4

Ingredients

- 4 chicken breast halves, skinless and boneless

- 1 cup extra virgin olive oil

- 1 lemon, juiced

- 2 teaspoons garlic, crushed

- 1 and 1/2 teaspoons black pepper

- 1/3 teaspoon paprika

Directions:

1. Cut 3 slits in the chicken breast

2. Take a small bowl and whisk in olive oil, salt, lemon juice, garlic, paprika, pepper and whisk for 30 seconds

3. Place chicken in a large bowl and pour marinade

4. Rub the marinade all over using your hand

5. Refrigerate overnight

6. Pre-heat grill to medium heat and oil the grate

7. Cook chicken in the grill until center is no longer pink

8. Serve and enjoy!

Nutrition: Calories: 644 Fat: 57g Carbs: 2g Protein: 27g Sugar: 14g; Fiber: 10g; Sodium: 140mg

25.   Chipotle Lettuce Chicken

Preparation Time: 10 minutes

Cooking Time: 25 minutes

Servings: 3

Ingredients

- 1 pound chicken breast, cut into strips

- Splash of olive oil

- 1 red onion, finely sliced

- 14 ounces tomatoes

- 1 teaspoon chipotle, chopped

- 1/2 teaspoon cumin

- Pinch of sugar

- Lettuce as needed

- Fresh coriander leaves

- Jalapeno chilies, sliced

- Fresh tomato slices for garnish

- Lime wedges

Directions:

1. Take a non-stick frying pan and place it over medium heat

2. Add oil and heat it up

3. Add chicken and cook until brown

4. Keep the chicken on the side

5. Add tomatoes, sugar, chipotle, cumin to the same pan and simmer for 25 minutes until you have a nice sauce

6. Add chicken into the sauce and cook for 5 minutes

7. Transfer the mix to another place

8. Use lettuce wraps to take a portion of the mixture and serve with a squeeze of lemon

9. Enjoy!

Nutrition: Calories: 332 Fat: 15g Carbs: 13g Protein: 34g Sugar: 12g; Fiber: 10g; Sodium: 140mg

26.   Stylish Chicken-Bacon Wrap

Preparation Time: 5 minutes

Cooking Time: 50 minutes

Servings: 3

Ingredients

- 8 ounces lean chicken breast

- 6 bacon slices

- 3 ounces shredded cheese

- 4 slices ham

Directions:

1. Cut chicken breast into bite-sized portions

2. Transfer shredded cheese onto ham slices

3. Roll up chicken breast and ham slices in bacon slices

4. Take a skillet and place it over medium heat

5. Add olive oil and brown bacon for a while

6. Remove rolls and transfer to your oven

7. Bake for 45 minutes at 325 degrees F

8. Serve and enjoy!

Nutrition: Calories: 275 Fat: 11g Carbs: 0.5g Protein: 40g Sugar: 14g; Fiber: 10g; Sodium: 138mg

27.   Healthy Cottage Cheese Pancakes

Preparation Time: 10 minutes

Cooking Time: 15

Servings: 1

Ingredients:

- 1/2 cup of Cottage cheese (low-fat)

- 1/3 cup (approx. 2 egg whites) Egg whites

- ¼ cup of Oats

- 1 teaspoon of Vanilla extract

- Olive oil cooking spray

- 1 tablespoon of Stevia (raw)

- Berries or sugar-free jam (optional)

Directions:

1. Begin by taking a food blender and adding in the egg whites and cottage cheese. Also add in the vanilla extract, a pinch of stevia, and oats. Palpitate until the consistency is well smooth.

2. Get a nonstick pan and oil it nicely with the cooking spray. Position the pan on low heat.

3. After it has been heated, scoop out half of the batter and pour it on the pan. Cook for about 2 1/2 minutes on each side.

4. Position the cooked pancakes on a serving plate and cover with sugar-free jam or berries.

Nutrition: Calories: 205 Fat: 1.5 g, Protein: 24.5 g, Carbs: 19 g Sugar: 14g; Fiber: 10g; Sodium: 140mg

28.   Avocado Lemon Toast

Preparation Time: 10 minutes

Cooking Time: 13 minutes

Servings: 2

Ingredients:

- Whole-grain bread: 2 slices

- Fresh cilantro (chopped): 2 tablespoons

- Lemon zest: ¼ teaspoon

- Fine sea salt: 1 pinch

Directions:

1. Begin by getting a medium-sized mixing bowl and adding in the avocado. Make use of a fork to crush it properly.

2. Then, add in the cilantro, lemon zest, lemon juice, sea salt, and cayenne pepper. Mix well until combined.

3. Toast the bread slices in a toaster until golden brown. It should take about 3 minutes.

4. Top the toasted bread slices with the avocado mixture and finalize by drizzling with chia seeds.

Nutrition: Calories: 72 Protein: 3.6 g Fat: 1.2 g Carbs: 11.6 g Sugar: 12g; Fiber: 8g; Sodium: 139mg

29.   Healthy Baked Eggs

Preparation Time: 10 minutes

Cooking Time: 1 hour

Servings: 3

Ingredients:

- Olive oil: 1 tablespoon

- Garlic: 2 cloves

- Eggs: 8 large

- Sea salt: 1/2 teaspoon

- Shredded mozzarella cheese (medium-fat): 3 cups

- Olive oil spray

- Onion (chopped): 1 medium

- Spinach leaves: 8 ounces

- Half-and-half: 1 cup

- Black pepper: 1 teaspoon

- Feta cheese: 1/2 cup

Directions:

1. Begin by heating the oven to 375F.

2. Get a glass baking dish and grease it with olive oil spray. Arrange aside.

3. Now take a nonstick pan and pour in the olive oil. Position the pan on allows heat and allows it heat.

4. Immediately you are done, toss in the garlic, spinach, and onion. Prepare for about 5 minutes. Arrange aside.

5. You can now Get a large mixing bowl and add in the half, eggs, pepper, and salt. Whisk thoroughly to combine.

6. Put in the feta cheese and chopped mozzarella cheese (reserve 1/2 cup of mozzarella cheese for later).

7. Put the egg mixture and prepared spinach to the prepared glass baking dish. Blend well to combine. Drizzle the reserved cheese over the top.

8. Bake the egg mix for about 45 minutes.

9. Extract the baking dish from the oven and allow it to stand for 10 minutes.

10. Dice and serve!

Nutrition: Calories: 323 Fat: 22.3 g Protein: 22.6 g Carbs: 7.9 g Sugar: 14g; Fiber: 12g; Sodium: 144mg

30.   Quick Low-Carb Oatmeal

Preparation Time: 10 minutes

Cooking Time: 15 minutes

Servings: 2

Ingredients:

- Almond flour: 1/2 cup

- Flax meal: 2 tablespoons

- Cinnamon (ground): 1 teaspoon

- Almond milk (unsweetened): 11/2 cups

- Salt: as per taste

- Chia seeds: 2 tablespoons

- Liquid stevia: 10: 15 drops

- Vanilla extract: 1 teaspoon

Directions:

1. Begin by taking a large mixing bowl and adding in the coconut flour, almond flour, ground cinnamon, flax seed powder, and chia seeds. Mix properly to combine.

2. Position a stockpot on a low heat and add in the dry ingredients. Also add in the liquid stevia, vanilla extract, and almond milk. Mix well to combine.

3. Prepare the flour and almond milk for about 4 minutes. Add salt if needed.

4. Move the oatmeal to a serving bowl and top with nuts, seeds, and pure and neat berries.

Nutrition: Calories: Protein: 11.7 g Fat: 24.3 g Carbs: 16.7 g Sugar: 13g; Fiber: 12g; Sodium: 135mg

31. Tofu and Vegetable Scramble

Preparation Time: 10 minutes

Cooking Time: 15 minutes

Servings: 2

Ingredients:

- Firm tofu (drained): 16 ounces

- Sea salt: 1/2 teaspoon

- Garlic powder: 1 teaspoon

- Fresh coriander: for garnishing

- Red onion: 1/2 medium

- Cumin powder: 1 teaspoon

- Lemon juice: for topping

- Green bell pepper: 1 medium

- Garlic powder: 1 teaspoon

- Fresh coriander: for garnishing

- Red onion: 1/2 medium

- Cumin powder: 1 teaspoon

- Lemon juice: for topping

Directions:

1. Begin by preparing the ingredients. For this, you are to extract the seeds of the tomato and green bell pepper. Shred the onion, bell pepper, and tomato into small cubes.

2. Get a small mixing bowl and position the fairly hard tofu inside it. Make use of your hands to break the fairly hard tofu. Arrange aside.

3. Get a nonstick pan and add in the onion, tomato, and bell pepper. Mix and cook for about 3 minutes.

4. Put the somewhat hard crumbled tofu to the pan and combine well.

5. Get a small bowl and put in the water, turmeric, garlic powder, cumin powder, and chili powder. Combine well and stream it over the tofu and vegetable mixture.

6. Allow the tofu and vegetable crumble cook with seasoning for 5 minutes. Continuously stir so that the pan is not holding the ingredients.

7. Drizzle the tofu scramble with chili flakes and salt. Combine well.

8. Transfer the prepared scramble to a serving bowl and give it a proper spray of lemon juice.

9. Finalize by garnishing with pure and neat coriander. Serve while hot!

Nutrition: Calories: 238 Carbs: 16.6 g Fat: 11 g Sugar: 13g; Fiber: 11g; Sodium: 142mg

32.   Breakfast Smoothie Bowl with Fresh Berries

Preparation Time: 10 minutes

Cooking Time: 5 minutes

Servings: 2

Ingredients

- 1 heaping cup organic frozen mixed berries

- 1 small ripe banana (sliced and frozen)

- 2-3 Tbsp light coconut or almond milk

Directions:

1. Begin by taking a blender and adding in the mashed ice cubes. Allow them to rest for about 30 seconds.

2. Then put in the almond milk, shredded strawberries, pea protein powder, psyllium husk powder, coconut oil, and liquid stevia. Blend well until it turns into a smooth and creamy puree.

3. Vacant the prepared smoothie into 2 glasses.

4. Cover with coconut flakes and pure and neat strawberries.

Nutrition: Calories: 166 Fat: 9.2 g Carbs: 4.1 g Protein: 17.6 g Sugar: 11g; Fiber: 13g; Sodium: 136mg

33.   Chia and Coconut Pudding

Preparation Time: 10 minutes

Cooking Time: 5 minutes

Servings: 2

Ingredients:

- Light coconut milk: 7 ounces

- Liquid stevia: 3 to 4 drops

- Kiwi: 1

- Chia seeds: ¼ cup

- Clementine: 1

- Shredded coconut (unsweetened)

Directions:

1. Begin by getting a mixing bowl and putting in the light coconut milk. Set in the liquid stevia to sweeten the milk. Combine well.

2. Put the chia seeds to the milk and whisk until well-combined. Arrange aside.

3. Scrape the clementine and carefully extract the skin from the wedges. Leave aside.

4. Also, scrape the kiwi and dice it into small pieces.

5. Get a glass vessel and gather the pudding. For this, position the fruits at the bottom of the jar; then put a dollop of chia pudding. Then spray the fruits and then put another layer of chia pudding.

6. Finalize by garnishing with the rest of the fruits and chopped coconut.

Nutrition: Calories: 201 Protein: 5.4 g Fat: 10 g Carbs: 22.8 g Sugar: 14g; Fiber: 10g; Sodium: 140mg

34. Tomato and Zucchini Sauté

Preparation Time: 10 minutes

Cooking Time: 43 minutes

Servings: 3

Ingredients:

- Vegetable oil: 1 tablespoon
- Tomatoes (chopped): 2
- Green bell pepper (chopped): 1
- Black pepper (freshly ground): as per taste
- Onion (sliced): 1
- Zucchini (peeled): 2 pounds and cut into 1-inch-thick slices
- Salt: as per taste
- Uncooked white rice: ¼ cup

Directions:

1. Begin by getting a nonstick pan and putting it over low heat. Stream in the oil and allow it to heat through.

Put in the onions and sauté for about 3 minutes.

2. Then pour in the zucchini and green peppers. Mix well and spice with black pepper and salt.

3. Reduce the heat and cover the pan with a lid. Allow the veggies cook on low for 5 minutes.

4. While you're done, put in the water and rice. Place the lid back on and cook on low for 20 minutes.

Nutrition: Calories: 94 Fat: 2.8 g Protein: 3.2 g Carbs: 16.1 g Sugar: 16g; Fiber: 9g; Sodium: 133mg

35. Steamed Kale with Mediterranean Dressing

Preparation Time: 10 minutes

Cooking Time: 25 minutes

Servings: 3

Ingredients:

- Kale (chopped): 12 cups
- Olive oil: 1 tablespoon
- Soy sauce: 1 teaspoon
- Pepper (freshly ground): as per taste
- Lemon juice: 2 tablespoons
- Garlic (minced): 1 tablespoon
- Salt: as per taste

Directions:

1. Get a gas steamer or an electric steamer and fill the bottom pan with water. If making use of a gas steamer, position it on high heat. Making use of an electric steamer, place it on the highest setting.

2. Immediately the water comes to a boil, put in the shredded kale and cover with a lid. Boil for about 8 minutes. The kale should be tender by now.

3. During the kale is boiling, take a big mixing bowl and put in the olive oil, lemon juice, soy sauce, garlic, pepper, and salt. Whisk well to mix.

4. Now toss in the steamed kale and carefully enclose into the dressing. Be assured the kale is well-coated.

5. Serve while it's hot!

Nutrition: Calories: 91 Fat: 3.5 g Protein: 4.6 g Carbs: 14.5 g Sugar: 14.2g; Fiber: 12.5g; Sodium: 139mg

Lunch Recipes

36. Cauliflower Rice with Chicken

Preparation Time: 15 Minutes

Cooking Time: 15 Minutes

Servings: 4

Ingredients

- 1/2 large cauliflower
- 3/4 cup cooked meat
- 1/2 bell pepper
- 1 carrot
- 2 ribs celery
- 1 tbsp. stir fry sauce (low carb)
- 1 tbsp. extra virgin olive oil
- Salt and pepper to taste

Directions

1. Chop cauliflower in a processor to "rice." Place in a bowl.

2. Properly chop all vegetables in a food processor into thin slices.

3. Add cauliflower and other plants to WOK with heated oil. Fry until all veggies are tender.

4. Add chopped meat and sauce to the wok and fry 10 Minutes.

5. Serve.

6. This dish is very mouth-watering!

Nutrition: Calories 200 Protein 10 g Fat 12 g Carbs 10 g Sugar: 14g; Fiber: 12g; Sodium: 143mg

37. Turkey with Fried Eggs

Preparation Time: 10 Minutes

Cooking Time: 20 Minutes Servings: 4

Ingredients

- 4 large potatoes
- 1 cooked turkey thigh
- 1 large onion (about 2 cups diced)
- butter
- Chile flakes
- 4 eggs
- salt to taste
- pepper to taste

Directions

1. Rub the cold boiled potatoes on the coarsest holes of a box grater. Dice the turkey.

2. Cook the onion in as much unsalted butter as you feel comfortable with until it's just fragrant and translucent.

3. Add the rubbed potatoes and a cup of diced cooked turkey, salt and pepper to taste, and cook 20 Minutes.

4. Top each with a fried egg. Yummy!

Nutrition: Calories 170 Protein 19 g Fat 7 g Carbs 6 g Sugar: 11g; Fiber: 13g; Sodium: 128mg

38. Sweet Potato, Kale, and White Bean Stew

Preparation time: 15 minutes

Cooking time: 25 minutes

Servings: 4

Ingredients:

- 1 (15-ounce) can low-sodium cannellini beans, rinsed and drained, divided
- 1 tablespoon olive oil
- 1 medium onion, chopped
- 2 garlic cloves, minced
- 2 celery stalks, chopped
- 3 medium carrots, chopped
- 2 cups low-sodium vegetable broth
- 1 teaspoon apple cider vinegar
- 2 medium sweet potatoes (about 1¼ pounds)
- 2 cups chopped kale
- 1 cup shelled edamame
- ¼ cup quinoa
- 1 teaspoon dried thyme
- 1/2 teaspoon cayenne pepper
- 1/2 teaspoon salt
- ¼ teaspoon freshly ground black pepper

Directions:

1. Put half the beans into a blender and blend until smooth. Set aside.

2. In a large soup pot over medium heat, heat the oil. When the oil is shining, include the onion and garlic, and cook until the onion softens and the garlic is sweet, about 3 minutes. Add the celery and carrots, and continue cooking until the vegetables soften, about 5 minutes.

3. Add the broth, vinegar, sweet potatoes, unblended beans, kale, edamame, and quinoa, and bring the mixture to a boil. Reduce the heat and simmer until the vegetables soften, about 10 minutes.

4. Add the blended beans, thyme, cayenne, salt, and black pepper, increase the heat to medium-high, and bring the mixture to a boil. Reduce the heat and simmer, uncovered, until the flavors combine, about 5 minutes.

5. Into each of 4 containers, scoop 1¾ cups of stew.

Nutrition: Calories: 373; Fat: 7g; Protein: 15g; Carbs: 65g; Fiber: 15g; Sugar: 13g; Sodium: 540mg

39. Slow Cooker Two-Bean Sloppy Joes

Preparation time: 10 minutes

Cooking time: 6 hours

Servings: 4

Ingredients:

- 1 (15-ounce) can low-sodium black beans
- 1 (15-ounce) can low-sodium pinto beans
- 1 (15-ounce) can no-salt-added diced tomatoes
- 1 medium green bell pepper, cored, seeded, and chopped
- 1 medium yellow onion, chopped
- ¼ cup low-sodium vegetable broth

- 2 garlic cloves, minced

- 2 servings (¼ cup) meal prep barbecue sauce or bottled barbecue sauce

- ¼ teaspoon salt

- ¼ teaspoon freshly ground black pepper

- 4 whole-wheat buns

Directions:

1. In a slow cooker, combine the black beans, pinto beans, diced tomatoes, bell pepper, onion, broth, garlic, meal prep barbecue sauce, salt, and black pepper. Stir the ingredients, then cover and cook on low for 6 hours.

2. Into each of 4 containers, spoon 1¼ cups of sloppy joe mix. Serve with 1 whole-wheat bun.

3. Storage: place airtight containers in the refrigerator for up to 1 week. To freeze, place freezer-safe containers in the freezer for up to 2 months. To defrost, refrigerate overnight. To reheat individual portions, microwave uncovered on high for 2 to 21/2 minutes. Alternatively, reheat the entire dish in a saucepan on the stove top. Bring the sloppy joes to a boil, then reduce the heat and simmer until heated through, 10 to 15 minutes. Serve with a whole-wheat bun.

Nutrition: Calories: 392; Fat: 3g; Protein: 17g; Carbs: 79g; Fiber: 19g; Sugar: 15g; Sodium: 759mg

40.   Lighter Eggplant Parmesan

Preparation time: 15 minutes

Cooking time: 35 minutes

Servings: 4

Ingredients:

- Nonstick cooking spray

- 3 eggs, beaten

- 1 tablespoon dried parsley

- 2 teaspoons ground oregano

- 1/8 teaspoon freshly ground black pepper

- 1 cup panko bread crumbs, preferably whole-wheat

- 1 large eggplant (about 2 pounds)

- 5 servings (21/2 cups) chunky tomato sauce or jarred low-sodium tomato sauce

- 1 cup part-skim mozzarella cheese

- ¼ cup grated parmesan cheese

Directions:

1. Preheat the oven to 450f. Coat a baking sheet with cooking spray.

2. In a medium bowl, whisk together the eggs, parsley, oregano, and pepper.

3. Pour the panko into a separate medium bowl.

4. Slice the eggplant into ¼-inch-thick slices. Dip each slice of eggplant into the egg mixture, shaking off the excess. Then dredge both sides of the eggplant in the panko bread crumbs. Place the coated eggplant on the prepared baking sheet, leaving a 1/2-inch space between each slice.

5. Bake for about 15 minutes until soft and golden brown. Remove from the oven and set aside to slightly cool.

6. Pour 1/2 cup of chunky tomato sauce on the bottom of an 8-by-15-inch baking dish. Using a spatula or the back of a spoon spread the tomato sauce evenly.

Place half the slices of cooked eggplant, slightly overlapping, in the dish, and top with 1 cup of chunky tomato sauce, 1/2 cup of mozzarella and 2 tablespoons of grated parmesan. Repeat the layer, ending with the cheese.

7. Bake uncovered for 20 minutes until the cheese is bubbling and slightly browned.

8. Remove from the oven and allow cooling for 15 minutes before dividing the eggplant equally into 4 separate containers.

Nutrition: Calories: 333; Fat: 14g; Protein: 20g; Carbs: 35g; Fiber: 11g; Sugar: 15g; Sodium: 994mg

41.   Coconut-Lentil Curry

Preparation time: 15 minutes

Cooking time: 35 minutes

Servings: 4

Ingredients:

- 1 tablespoon olive oil

- 1 medium yellow onion, chopped

- 1 garlic clove, minced

- 1 medium red bell pepper, diced

- 1 (15-ounce) can green or brown lentils, rinsed and drained

- 2 medium sweet potatoes, washed, peeled, and cut into bite-size chunks (about 1¼ pounds)

- 1 (15-ounce) can no-salt-added diced tomatoes

- 2 tablespoons tomato paste

- 4 teaspoons curry powder

- 1/8 teaspoon ground cloves

- 1 (15-ounce) can light coconut milk

- ¼ teaspoon salt

- 2 pieces whole-wheat naan bread, halved, or 4 slices crusty bread

Directions:

1. In a large saucepan over medium heat, heat the olive oil. When the oil is shimmering, add both the onion and garlic and cook until the onion softens and the garlic is sweet, for about 3 minutes.

2. Add the bell pepper and continue cooking until it softens, about 5 minutes more. Add the lentils, sweet potatoes, tomatoes, tomato paste, curry powder, and cloves, and bring the mixture to a boil. Reduce the heat to medium-low, cover, and simmer until the potatoes are softened, about 20 minutes.

3. Add the coconut milk and salt, and return to a boil. Reduce the heat and simmer until the flavors combine, about 5 minutes.

4. Into each of 4 containers, spoon 2 cups of curry.

5. Enjoy each serving with half of a piece of naan bread or 1 slice of crusty bread.

Nutrition: Calories: 559; Fat: 16g; Protein: 16g; Carbs: 86g; Fiber: 16g; Sugar: 18g; Sodium: 819mg

42.   Stuffed Portobello with Cheese

Preparation time: 15 minutes

Cooking time: 25 minutes

Servings: 4

Ingredients:

- 4 Portobello mushroom caps
- 1 tablespoon olive oil
- 1/2 teaspoon salt, divided
- ¼ teaspoon freshly ground black pepper, divided
- 1 cup baby spinach, chopped
- 1 1/2 cups part-skim ricotta cheese
- 1/2 cup part-skim shredded mozzarella cheese
- ¼ cup grated parmesan cheese
- 1 garlic clove, minced
- 1 tablespoon dried parsley
- 2 teaspoons dried oregano
- 4 teaspoons unseasoned bread crumbs, divided
- 4 servings (4 cups) roasted broccoli with shallots

Directions:

1. Preheat the oven to 375f. Line a baking sheet with aluminum foil.

2. Brush the mushroom caps with the olive oil, and sprinkle with ¼ teaspoon salt and 1/8 teaspoon pepper. Put the mushroom caps on the prepared baking sheet and bake until soft, about 12 minutes.

3. In a medium bowl, mix together the spinach, ricotta, mozzarella, parmesan, garlic, parsley, oregano, and the remaining ¼ teaspoon of salt and 1/8 teaspoon of pepper.

4. Spoon 1/2 cup of cheese mixture into each mushroom cap, and sprinkle each with 1 teaspoon of bread crumbs. Return

the mushrooms to the oven for an additional 8 to 10 minutes until warmed through.

5. Remove from the oven and allow the mushrooms to cool for about 10 minutes before placing each in an individual container. Add 1 cup of roasted broccoli with shallots to each container.

Nutrition: Calories: 419; Fat: 30g; Protein: 23g; Carbs: 19g; Fiber: 2g; Sugar: 3g; Sodium: 790mg

43. Lighter Shrimp Scampi

Preparation time: 15 minutes

Cooking time: 15 minutes

Servings: 4

Ingredients:

- 1 1/2 pounds large peeled and deveined shrimp
- ¼ teaspoon salt
- 1/8 teaspoon freshly ground black pepper
- 2 tablespoons olive oil
- 1 shallot, chopped
- 2 garlic cloves, minced
- ¼ cup cooking white wine
- Juice of 1/2 lemon (1 tablespoon)
- 1/2 teaspoon sriracha
- 2 tablespoons unsalted butter, at room temperature
- ¼ cup chopped fresh parsley
- 4 servings (6 cups) zucchini noodles with lemon vinaigrette

Directions:

1. Season the shrimp with the salt and pepper.

2. In a medium saucepan over medium heat, heat the oil. Add the shallot and garlic, and cook until the shallot softens and the garlic is fragrant, about 3 minutes. Add the shrimp, cover, and cook until opaque, 2 to 3 minutes on each side. Using a slotted spoon, transfer the shrimp to a large plate.

3. Add the wine, lemon juice, and sriracha to the saucepan, and stir to combine. Bring the mixture to a boil, then reduce the heat and simmer until the liquid is reduced by about half, 3 minutes. Add the butter and stir until melted, about 3 minutes. Return the shrimp to the saucepan and toss to coat. Add the parsley and stir to combine.

4. Into each of 4 containers, place 1 1/2 cups of zucchini noodles with lemon vinaigrette, and top with ¾ cup of scampi.

Nutrition: Calories: 364; Fat: 21g; Protein: 37g; Carbs: 10g; Fiber: 2g; Sugar: 6g; Sodium: 557mg

44.   Maple-Mustard Salmon

Preparation time: 10 minutes, plus 30 minutes marinating time

Cooking time: 20 minutes

Servings: 4

Ingredients:

- Nonstick cooking spray

- 1/2 cup 100% maple syrup

- 2 tablespoons Dijon mustard

- ¼ teaspoon salt

- 4 (5-ounce) salmon fillets

- 4 servings (4 cups) roasted broccoli with shallots

- 4 servings (2 cups) parleyed whole-wheat couscous

Directions:

1. Preheat the oven to 400f. Line a baking sheet with aluminum foil and coat with cooking spray.

2. In a medium bowl, whisk together the maple syrup, mustard, and salt until smooth.

3. Put the salmon fillets into the bowl and toss to coat. Cover and place in the refrigerator to marinate for at least 30 minutes and up to overnight.

4. Shake off excess marinade from the salmon fillets and place them on the prepared baking sheet, leaving a 1-inch space between each fillet. Discard the extra marinade.

5. Bake for about 20 minutes until the salmon is opaque and a thermometer inserted in the thickest part of a fillet reads 145f.

6. Into each of 4 resealable containers, place 1 salmon fillet, 1 cup of roasted broccoli with shallots, and 1/2 cup of parleyed whole-wheat couscous.

Nutrition: Calories: 601; Fat: 29g; Protein: 36g; Carbs: 51g; Fiber: 3g; Sugar: 23g; Sodium: 610mg

45.   Chicken Salad with Grapes and Pecans

Preparation Time: 15 Minutes

Cooking Time: 5 Minutes

Servings: 4

Ingredients:

- 1/3 cup unsalted pecans, chopped
- 10 ounces cooked skinless, boneless chicken breast or rotisserie chicken, finely chopped
- 1/2 medium yellow onion, finely chopped
- 1 celery stalk, finely chopped
- ¾ cup red or green seedless grapes, halved
- ¼ cup light mayonnaise
- ¼ cup nonfat plain Greek yogurt
- 1 tablespoon Dijon mustard
- 1 tablespoon dried parsley
- ¼ teaspoon salt
- 1/8 teaspoon freshly ground black pepper
- 1 cup shredded romaine lettuce
- 4 (8-inch) whole-wheat pitas

Directions:

1. Heat a small skillet over medium-low heat to toast the pecans. Cook the pecans until fragrant, about 3 minutes. Remove from the heat and set aside to cool.

2. In a medium bowl, mix the chicken, onion, celery, pecans, and grapes.

3. In a small bowl, whisk together the mayonnaise, yogurt, mustard, parsley, salt, and pepper. Spoon the sauce over the chicken mixture and stir until well combined.

4. Into each of 4 containers, place ¼ cup of lettuce and top with 1 cup of chicken

salad. Store the pitas separately until ready to serve.

5. When ready to eat, stuff the serving of salad and lettuce into 1 pita.

Nutrition: Calories 163 Fat 4.2 g Carbs 22.5 g Fiber 6.3 g Sugar 2.3 g Protein 9.2 g Sodium 861 mg

46.   Roasted Vegetables

Preparation time: 14 minutes

Cooking time: 17 minutes

Servings: 3

Ingredients:

- 4 Tbsp. olive oil, reserve some for greasing
- 2 heads, large garlic, tops sliced off
- 2 large eggplants/aubergine, tops removed, cubed
- 2 large shallots, peeled, quartered
- 1 large carrot, peeled, cubed
- 1 large parsnips, peeled, cubed
- 1 small green bell pepper, deseeded, ribbed, cubed
- 1 small red bell pepper, deseeded, ribbed, cubed
- ½ pound Brussels sprouts, halved, do not remove cores
- 1 sprig, large thyme, leaves picked
- sea salt, coarse-grained

For garnish

- 1 large lemon, halved, ½ squeezed, ½ sliced into smaller wedges

51

- ⅛ cup fennel bulb, minced

Directions:

1. From 425°F or 220°C preheat oven for at least 5 minutes before using.

2. Line deep roasting pan with aluminum foil; lightly grease with oil. Tumble in bell peppers, Brussels sprouts, carrots, eggplants, garlic, parsnips, rosemary leaves, shallots, and thyme. Add a pinch of sea salt; drizzle in remaining oil and lemon juice. Toss well to combine.

3. Cover roasting pan with a sheet of aluminum foil. Place this on middle rack of oven. Bake for 20 to 30 minutes. Remove aluminum foil. Roast, for another 5 to 10 minutes, or until some vegetables brown at the edges. Remove roasting pan from oven. Cool slightly before ladling equal portions into plates.

4. Garnish with fennel and a wedge of lemon. Squeeze lemon juice on top of dish before eating.

Nutrition: Calories: 270 Fat: 8g Carbs: 42g Fiber: 5g Sugar: 3g Protein: 6g Sodium 320 mg

47.   Millet Pilaf

Preparation time: 10 minutes

Cooking time: 15 minutes

Servings: 4

Ingredients:

- 1 cup millet

- 2 tomatoes, rinsed, seeded, and chopped

- 1¾ cups filtered water

- 2 tablespoons extra-virgin olive oil

- ¼ cup chopped dried apricot

- Zest of 1 lemon

- Juice of 1 lemon

- ½ cup fresh parsley, rinsed and chopped

- Himalayan pink salt

- Freshly ground black pepper

Directions:

1. In an electric pressure cooker, combine the millet, tomatoes, and water. Lock the lid into place, select Manual and High Pressure, and cook for 7 minutes.

2. When the beep sounds, quick release the pressure by pressing Cancel and twisting the steam valve to the Venting position. Carefully remove the lid.

3. Stir in the olive oil, apricot, lemon zest, lemon juice, and parsley. Taste, season with salt and pepper, and serve.

Nutrition: Calories 203 Fat 41.2 g Carbs 29.5 g Fiber 16.3 g Sugar 29.3 g Protein 19.2 g Sodium 154mg

48.   Sweet and Sour Onions

Preparation time: 10 minutes

Cooking time: 11 minutes

Servings: 4

Ingredients:

- 4 large onions, halved

- 2 garlic cloves, crushed

- 3 cups vegetable stock

- 1 ½ tablespoon balsamic vinegar

- ½ teaspoon Dijon mustard

- 1 tablespoon sugar

Directions:

1. Combine onions and garlic in a pan. Fry for 3 minutes, or till softened.

2. Pour stock, vinegar, Dijon mustard, and sugar. Bring to a boil.

3. Reduce heat. Cover and let the combination simmer for 10 minutes.

4. Get rid of from heat. Continue stirring until the liquid is reduced and the onions are brown. Serve.

Nutrition: Calories 343 Fat 51.2 g Carbs 22.5 g Fiber 6.3 g Sugar 2.3 g Protein 9.2 g Sodium 135mg

49. Sautéed Apples and Onions

Preparation time: 14 minutes

Cooking time: 16 minutes

Servings: 3

Ingredients:

*   2 cups dry cider

*   1 large onion, halved

*   2 cups vegetable stock

*   4 apples, sliced into wedges

*   Pinch of salt

*   Pinch of pepper

Directions:

1. Combine cider and onion in a saucepan. Bring to a boil until the onions are cooked and liquid almost gone.

2. Pour the stock and the apples. Season with salt and pepper. Stir occasionally. Cook for about 10 minutes or until the apples are tender but not mushy. Serve.

Nutrition: Calories 163 Fat 4.2 g Carbs 22.5 g Fiber 6.3 g Sugar 2.3 g Protein 9.2 g Sodium 112mg

50. Zucchini Noodles with Portabella Mushrooms

Preparation time: 14 minutes

Cooking time: 16 minutes

Servings: 3

Ingredients:

*   1 zucchini, processed into spaghetti-like noodles

*   3 garlic cloves, minced

*   2 white onions, thinly sliced

*   1 thumb-sized ginger, julienned

*   1 lb. chicken thighs

*   1 lb. portabella mushrooms, sliced into thick slivers

*   2 cups chicken stock

*   3 cups water

*   Pinch of sea salt, add more if needed

*   Pinch of black pepper, add more if needed

*   2 tsp. sesame oil

*   4 Tbsp. coconut oil, divided

*   ¼ cup fresh chives, minced, for garnish

Directions:

1. Pour 2 tablespoons of coconut oil into a large saucepan. Fry mushroom slivers in batches for 5 minutes or until seared

brown. Set aside. Transfer these to a plate.

2. Sauté the onion, garlic, and ginger for 3 minutes or until tender. Add in chicken thighs, cooked mushrooms, chicken stock, water, salt, and pepper stir mixture well. Bring to a boil.

3. Decrease gradually the heat and allow simmering for 20 minutes or until the chicken is forking tender. Tip in sesame oil.

4. Serve by placing an equal amount of zucchini noodles into bowls. Ladle soup and garnish with chives.

Nutrition: Calories 163 Fat 4.2 g Carbs 22.5 g Fiber 6.3 g Sugar 2.3 g Protein 9.2 g Sodium 130mg

51.   Grilled Tempeh with Pineapple

Preparation time: 12 minutes

Cooking time: 16 minutes

Servings: 3

Ingredients:

- 10 oz. tempeh, sliced

- 1 red bell pepper, quartered

- 1/4 pineapple, sliced into rings

- 6 oz. green beans

- 1 tbsp. coconut aminos

- 2 1/2 tbsp. orange juice, freshly squeeze

- 1 1/2 tbsp. lemon juice, freshly squeezed

- 1 tbsp. extra virgin olive oil

- 1/4 cup hoisin sauce

Directions:

1. Blend together the olive oil, orange and lemon juices, coconut aminos or soy sauce, and hoisin sauce in a bowl. Add the diced tempeh and set aside.

2. Heat up the grill or place a grill pan over medium high flame. Once hot, lift the marinated tempeh from the bowl with a pair of tongs and transfer them to the grill or pan.

3. Grille for 2 to 3 minutes, or until browned all over.

4. Grill the sliced pineapples alongside the tempeh, then transfer them directly onto the serving platter.

5. Place the grilled tempeh beside the grilled pineapple and cover with aluminum foil to keep warm.

6. Meanwhile, place the green beans and bell peppers in a bowl and add just enough of the marinade to coat.

7. Prepare the grill pan and add the vegetables. Grill until fork tender and slightly charred.

8. Transfer the grilled vegetables to the serving platter and arrange artfully with the tempeh and pineapple. Serve at once.

Nutrition: Calories 173 Fat 9.2 g Carbs 22.5 g Fiber 6.3 g Sugar 2.3 g Protein 9.2 g Sodium 105mg

52.   Zucchini Courgettes In Cider Sauce

Preparation time: 13 minutes

Cooking time: 17 minutes

Servings: 3

Ingredients:

- 2 cups baby courgettes

- 3 tablespoons vegetable stock

- 2 tablespoons apple cider vinegar

- 1 tablespoon light brown sugar

- 4 spring onions, finely sliced

- 1 piece fresh gingerroot, grated

- 1 teaspoon corn flour

- 2 teaspoons water

Directions:

1. Bring a pan with salted water to a boil. Add courgettes. Bring to a boil for 5 minutes.

2. Meanwhile, in a pan, combine vegetable stock, apple cider vinegar, brown sugar, onions, gingerroot, lemon juice and rind, and orange juice and rind. Take to a boil. Lower the heat and allow simmering for 3 minutes.

3. Mix the corn flour with water. Stir well. Pour into the sauce. Continue stirring until the sauce thickens.

4. Drain courgettes. Transfer to the serving dish. Spoon over the sauce. Toss to coat courgettes. Serve.

Nutrition: Calories 343 Fat 4.2 g Carbs 22.5 g Fiber 6.3 g Sugar 2.3 g Protein 9.2 g Sodium 135mg

53.   Baked Mixed Mushrooms

Preparation time: 8 minutes

Cooking time: 20 minutes

Servings: 3

Ingredients:

- 2 cups mixed wild mushrooms

- 1 cup chestnut mushrooms

- 2 cups dried porcini

- 2 shallots

- 4 garlic cloves

- 3 cups raw pecans

- ½ bunch fresh thyme

- 1 bunch flat-leaf parsley

- 2 tablespoons olive oil

- 2 fresh bay leaves

- 1 ½ cups stale bread

Directions:

1. Remove skin and finely chop garlic and shallots. Roughly chop the wild mushrooms and chestnut mushrooms. Pick the leaves of the thyme and tear the bread into small pieces. Put inside the pressure cooker.

2. Place the pecans and roughly chop the nuts. Pick the parsley leaves and roughly chop.

3. Place the porcini in a bowl then add 300ml of boiling water. Set aside until needed.

4. Heat oil in the pressure cooker. Add the garlic and shallots. Cook for 3 minutes while stirring occasionally.

5. Drain porcini and reserve the liquid. Add the porcini into the pressure cooker together with the wild mushrooms and chestnut mushrooms. Add the bay leaves and thyme.

6. Position the lid and lock in place. Put to high heat and bring to high pressure. Adjust heat to stabilize. Cook for 10 minutes. Adjust taste if necessary.

7. Transfer the mushroom mixture into a bowl and set aside to cool completely.

8. Once the mushrooms are completely cool, add the bread, pecans, a pinch of black pepper and sea salt, and half of the reserved liquid into the bowl. Mix well. Add more reserved liquid if the mixture seems dry.

9. Add more than half of the parsley into the bowl and stir. Transfer the mixture into a 20cm x 25cm lightly greased baking dish and cover with tin foil.

10. Bake in the oven for 35 minutes. Then, get rid of the foil and cook for another 10 minutes. Once done, sprinkle the remaining parsley on top and serve with bread or crackers. Serve.

Nutrition: Calories 163 Fat 4.2 g Carbs 22.5 g Fiber 6.3 g Sugar 2.3 g Protein 9.2 g Sodium 143mg

54.   Spiced Okra

Preparation time: 14 minutes

Cooking time: 16 minutes

Servings: 3

Ingredients:

- 2 cups okra
- ¼ teaspoon stevia
- 1 teaspoon chilli powder
- ½ teaspoon ground turmeric
- 1 tablespoon ground coriander
- 2 tablespoons fresh coriander, chopped
- 1 tablespoon ground cumin
- ¼ teaspoon salt
- 1 tablespoon desiccated coconut
- 3 tablespoons vegetable oil
- ½ teaspoon black mustard seeds
- ½ teaspoon cumin seeds
- Fresh tomatoes, to garnish

Directions:

1. Trim okra. Wash and dry.

2. Combine stevia, chilli powder, turmeric, ground coriander, fresh coriander, cumin, salt, and desiccated coconut in a bowl.

3. Heat the oil in a pan. Cook mustard and cumin seeds for 3 minutes. Stir continuously. Add okra. Tip in the spice mixture. Cook on low heat for 8 minutes.

4. Transfer to a serving dish. Garnish with fresh tomatoes.

Nutrition: Calories 131 Protein 12 Fat 1 g Carbs 19 g Sugar: 6g; Fiber: 7g; Sodium: 173mg

55.   Lemony Salmon Burgers

Preparation Time: 10 Minutes

Cooking Time: 10 Minutes

Servings: 4

Ingredients

- 2 (3-oz) cans boneless, skinless pink salmon
- 1/4 cup panko breadcrumbs
- 4 tsp. lemon juice
- 1/4 cup red bell pepper
- 1/4 cup sugar-free yogurt
- 1 egg

- 2 (1.5-oz) whole wheat hamburger toasted buns

Directions

1. Mix drained and flaked salmon, finely-chopped bell pepper, panko breadcrumbs.

2. Combine 2 tbsp. cup sugar-free yogurt, 3 tsp. fresh lemon juice, and egg in a bowl. Shape mixture into 2 (3-inch) patties, bake on the skillet over medium heat 4 to 5 Minutes per side.

3. Stir together 2 tbsp. sugar-free yogurt and 1 tsp. lemon juice; spread over bottom halves of buns.

4. Top each with 1 patty, and cover with bun tops.

5. This dish is very mouth-watering!

Nutrition: Calories 180 Protein 7 g Fat 4 g Carbs 20 g Sugar: 6g; Fiber: 9g; Sodium: 395mg

56.   Caprese Turkey Burgers

Preparation Time 10 Minutes

Cooking Time: 10 Minutes

Servings: 4

Ingredients

- 1/2 lb. 93% lean ground turkey

- 2 (1,5-oz) whole wheat hamburger buns (toasted)

- 1/4 cup shredded mozzarella cheese (part-skim)

- 1 egg

- 1 big tomato

- 1 small clove garlic

- 4 large basil leaves

- 1/8 tsp. salt

- 1/8 tsp. pepper

Directions

1. Combine turkey, white egg, Minced garlic, salt, and pepper (mix until combined);

2. Shape into 2 cutlets. Put cutlets into a skillet; cook 5 to 7 Minutes per side.

3. Top cutlets properly with cheese and sliced tomato at the end of cooking.

4. Put 1 cutlet on the bottom of each bun.

5. Top each patty with 2 basil leaves. Cover with bun tops.

My guests enjoy this dish every time they visit my home.

Nutrition: Calories 200 Protein 15 g Fat 3 g Carbs 6 g Sugar: 6g; Fiber: 5g; Sodium: 583mg

57.   Pasta Salad

Preparation Time: 15 Minutes

Cooking Time: 15 Minutes

Servings: 4

Ingredients

- 8 oz. whole-wheat pasta

- 2 tomatoes

- 1 (5-oz) pkg spring mix

- 9 slices bacon

- 1/3 cup mayonnaise (reduced-fat)

- 1 tbsp. Dijon mustard

- 3 tbsp. apple cider vinegar

- 1/4 tsp. salt

- 1/2 tsp. pepper

Directions

1. Cook pasta.

2. Chilled pasta, chopped tomatoes and spring mix in a bowl.

3. Crumble cooked bacon over pasta.

4. Combine mayonnaise, mustard, vinegar, salt and pepper in a small bowl.

5. Pour dressing over pasta, stirring to coat.

Understanding diabetes is the first step in curing.

Nutrition: Calories 150 Protein 15 g Fat 10 g Carbs 5 g Sugar: 6g; Fiber: 7g; Sodium: 489mg

58. Chicken, Strawberry, And Avocado Salad

Preparation Time: 10 Minutes

Cooking Time: 5 Minutes

Ingredients

- 1,5 cups chicken (skin removed)

- 1/4 cup almonds

- 2 (5-oz) pkg salad greens

- 1 (16-oz) pkg strawberries

- 1 avocado

- 1/4 cup green onion

- 1/4 cup lime juice

- 3 tbsp. extra virgin olive oil

- 2 tbsp. honey

- 1/4 tsp. salt

- 1/4 tsp. pepper

Directions

1. Toast almonds until golden and fragrant.

2. Mix lime juice, oil, honey, salt, and pepper.

3. Mix greens, sliced strawberries, chicken, diced avocado, and sliced green onion and sliced almonds; drizzle with dressing. Toss to coat.

4. Yummy!

Nutrition: Calories 40 Protein 10 g Fat 6 g Carbs 2 g Sugar: 6g; Fiber: 7g; Sodium: 773mg

59. Lemon-Thyme Eggs

Preparation Time: 10 Minutes

Cooking Time: 5 Minutes

Servings: 4

Ingredients

- 7 large eggs

- 1/4 cup mayonnaise (reduced-fat)

- 2 tsp. lemon juice

- 1 tsp. Dijon mustard

- 1 tsp. chopped fresh thyme

- 1/8 tsp. cayenne pepper

Directions

1. Bring eggs to a boil.

2. Peel and cut each egg in half lengthwise.

3. Remove yolks to a bowl. Add mayonnaise, lemon juice, mustard, thyme, and cayenne to egg yolks; mash to blend. Fill egg white halves with yolk mixture.

4. Chill until ready to serve.

5. Please your family with a delicious meal.

Nutrition: Calories 110 Protein 6 g Fat 2 g Carbs 1 g Sugar: 8g; Fiber: 10g; Sodium: 709mg

60.   Spinach Salad with Bacon

Preparation Time: 15 Minutes

Cooking Time: 0 Minutes

Servings: 4

Ingredients

- 8 slices center-cut bacon

- 3 tbsp. extra virgin olive oil

- 1 (5-oz) pkg baby spinach

- 1 tbsp. apple cider vinegar

- 1 tsp. Dijon mustard

- 1/2 tsp. honey

- 1/4 tsp. salt

- 1/2 tsp. pepper

Directions

1. Mix vinegar, mustard, honey, salt and pepper in a bowl.

2. Whisk in oil. Place spinach in a serving bowl; drizzle with dressing, and toss to coat.

3. Sprinkle with cooked and crumbled bacon.

Nutrition: Calories 110 Protein 6 g Fat 2 g Carbs 1 g

61.   Pea and Collards Soup

Preparation Time: 10 Minutes

Cooking Time: 50 Minutes

Servings: 4

Ingredients

- 1/2 (16-oz) pkg black-eyed peas

- 1 onion

- 2 carrots

- 1,5 cups ham (low-sodium)

- 1 (1-lb) bunch collard greens (trimmed)

- 1 tbsp. extra virgin olive oil

- 2 cloves garlic

- 1/2 tsp. black pepper

- Hot sauce

Directions

1. Cook chopped onion and carrots 10 Minutes.

2. Add peas, diced ham, collards, and Minced garlic. Cook 5 Minutes.

3. Add broth, 3 cups water, and pepper. Bring to a boil; simmer 35 Minutes, adding water if needed.

4. Serve with favorite sauce.

Nutrition: Calories 200 Protein 10 g Fat 20 g Carbs 1 g Sugar: 8g; Fiber: 7g; Sodium: 546mg

62.   Spanish Stew

Preparation Time: 10 Minutes

Cooking Time: 25 Minutes

Servings: 4

Ingredients

- 1.1/2 (12-oz) pkg smoked chicken sausage links

- 1 (5-oz) pkg baby spinach

- 1 (15-oz) can chickpeas

- 1 (14.5-oz) can tomatoes with basil, garlic, and oregano

- 1/2 tsp. smoked paprika

- 1/2 tsp. cumin

- 3/4 cup onions

- 1 tbsp. extra virgin olive oil

Directions

1. Cook sliced the sausage in hot oil until browned. Remove from pot.

2. Add chopped onions; cook until tender.

3. Add sausage, drained and rinsed chickpeas, diced tomatoes, paprika, and ground cumin. Cook 15 Minutes.

4. Add in spinach; cook 1 to 2 Minutes.

5. This dish is ideal for every day and for a festive table.

Nutrition: Calories 60 Protein 3 g Fat 1 g Carbs 8 g Sugar: 6g; Fiber: 7g; Sodium: 773mg

63.   Creamy Taco Soup

Preparation Time: 10 Minutes

Cooking Time: 20 Minutes

Servings: 4

Ingredients

- 3/4 lb. ground sirloin

- 1/2 (8-oz) cream cheese

- 1/2 onion

- 1 clove garlic

- 1 (10-oz) can tomatoes and green chiles

- 1 (14.5-oz) can beef broth

- 1/4 cup heavy cream

- 1,5 tsp. cumin

- 1/2 tsp. chili powder

Directions

1. Cook beef, chopped onion, and Minced garlic until meat is browned and crumbly; drain and return to pot.

2. Add ground cumin, chili powder, and cream cheese cut into small pieces and softened, stirring until cheese is melted.

3. Add diced tomatoes, broth, and cream; bring to a boil, and simmer 10 Minutes. Season with pepper and salt to taste.

4. You've got to give someone the recipe for this soup dish!

Nutrition: Calories 210 Protein 28 g Fat 17 g Carbs 0, 1 g Sugar: 5g; Fiber: 8g; Sodium: 674mg

64. Chicken with Caprese Salsa

Preparation Time: 15 Minutes

Cooking Time: 5 Minutes

Servings: 4

Ingredients

- 3/4 lb. boneless, skinless chicken breasts
- 2 big tomatoes
- 1/2 (8-oz) ball fresh mozzarella cheese
- 1/4 cup red onion
- 2 tbsp. fresh basil
- 1 tbsp. balsamic vinegar
- 2 tbsp. extra virgin olive oil (divided)
- 1/2 tsp. salt (divided)
- 1/4 tsp. pepper (divided)

Directions

1. Sprinkle cut in half lengthwise chicken with 1/4 tsp. salt and 1/8 tsp. pepper.
2. Heat 1 tbsp. olive oil, cook chicken 5 Minutes.
3. Meanwhile, mix chopped tomatoes, diced cheese, finely chopped onion, chopped basil, vinegar, 1 tbsp. oil, and 1/4 tsp. salt and 1/8 tsp. pepper.
4. Spoon salsa over chicken.
5. Chicken with Caprese Salsa is a nutritious, simple and very tasty dish that can be prepared in a few Minutes.

Nutrition: Calories 27 Protein 3 g Fat 0, 3 g Carbs 4 g Sugar: 11g; Fiber: 9g; Sodium: 644mg

65. Balsamic-Roasted Broccoli

Preparation Time: 10 Minutes

Cooking Time: 15 Minutes

Servings: 4

Ingredients

- 1 lb. broccoli
- 1 tbsp. extra virgin olive oil
- 1 tbsp. balsamic vinegar
- 1 clove garlic
- 1/8 tsp. salt
- Pepper to taste

Directions

1. Preheat oven to 450F.
2. Combine broccoli, olive oil, vinegar, Minced garlic, salt, and pepper; toss.
3. Spread broccoli on a baking sheet.
4. Bake 12 to 15 Minutes.
5. Really good!

Nutrition: Calories 170 Protein 17 g Fat 8 g Carbs 3 g Sugar: 6g; Fiber: 10g; Sodium: 681mg

66. Hearty Beef and Vegetable Soup

Preparation Time: 10 Minutes

Cooking Time: 30 Minutes

Servings: 4

Ingredients

- 1/2 lb. lean ground beef
- 2 cups beef broth
- 1,5 tbsp. vegetable oil (divided)
- 1 cup green bell pepper
- 1/2 cup red onion
- 1 cup green cabbage
- 1 cup frozen mixed vegetables
- 1/2 can tomatoes
- 1,5 tsp. Worcestershire sauce
- 1 small bay leaf
- 1,8 tsp. pepper
- 2 tbsp. ketchup

Directions

1. Cook beef in 1/2 tbsp. hot oil 2 Minutes.
2. Stir in chopped bell pepper and chopped onion; cook 4 Minutes.
3. Add chopped cabbage, mixed vegetables, stewed tomatoes, broth, Worcestershire sauce, bay leaf, and pepper; bring to a boil.
4. Reduce heat to medium; cover, and cook 15 Minutes.
5. Stir in ketchup and 1 tbsp. oil, and remove from heat. Let stand 10 Minutes.
6. The right diet is excellent diabetes remedy.

Nutrition: Calories 116 Protein 10 g Fat 7 g Carbs 3 g Sugar: 9g; Fiber: 17g; Sodium: 549mg

67.   Cauliflower Muffin

Preparation Time: 15 Minutes

Cooking Time: 30 Minutes

Servings: 4

Ingredients

- 2,5 cup cauliflower
- 2/3 cup ham
- 2,5 cups of cheese
- 2/3 cup champignon
- 1,5 tbsp. flaxseed
- 3 eggs
- 1/4 tsp. salt
- 1/8 tsp. pepper

Directions

1. 1. Preheat oven to 375 F.
2. Put muffin liners in a 12-muffin tin.
3. Combine diced cauliflower, ground flaxseed, beaten eggs, cup diced ham, grated cheese, and diced mushrooms, salt, pepper.
4. Divide mixture rightly between muffin liners.
5. Bake 30 Minutes.
6. This is a great lunch for the whole family.

Nutrition: Calories 180 Protein 13 g Fat 13 g Carbs 2 g Sugar: 6g; Fiber: 7g; Sodium: 773mg g

68.   Ham and Egg Cups

Preparation Time: 10 Minutes

Cooking Time: 15 Minutes

Servings: 4

Ingredients

- 5 slices ham
- 4 tbsp. cheese
- 1,5 tbsp. cream
- 3 egg whites
- 1,5 tbsp. pepper (green)
- 1 tsp. salt
- pepper to taste

Directions

1. Preheat oven to 350 F.
2. Arrange each slice of thinly sliced ham into 4 muffin tin.
3. Put 1/4 of grated cheese into ham cup.
4. Mix eggs, cream, salt and pepper and divide it into 2 tins.
5. Bake in oven 15 Minutes; after baking, sprinkle with green onions.
6. If you want to keep your current shape, also pay attention to this dish.

Nutrition: Calories: 1124 Fat: 72g Carbs: 59g Protein: 49g Sugar: 11g Fiber: 10g; Sodium: 140mg

69.   Bacon BBQ

Preparation time: 2 minutes

Cooking time: 8 minutes

Servings: 2

Ingredients:

- 13g dark brown sugar
- 5g chili powder
- 1g ground cumin
- 1g cayenne pepper
- 4 slices of bacon, cut in half

Directions:

1. Mix seasonings until well combined.
2. Dip the bacon in the dressing until it is completely covered. Leave aside.
3. Preheat the air fryer, set it to 160C.
4. Place the bacon in the preheated air fryer
5. Select Bacon and press Start/Pause.

Nutrition: Calories: 340 Fat: 15g Carbs: 32g Protein: 15g Sugar: 0g Fiber: 12g; Sodium: 128mg

70.   Misto Quente

Preparation time: 5 minutes

Cooking time: 10 minutes

Servings: 4

Ingredients:

- 4 slices of bread without shell
- 4 slices of turkey breast
- 4 slices of cheese
- 2 tbsp. cream cheese
- 2 spoons of butter

Directions:

1. Preheat the air fryer. Set the timer of 5 minutes and the temperature to 200C.

2. Pass the butter on one side of the slice of bread, and on the other side of the slice, the cream cheese.

3. Mount the sandwiches placing two slices of turkey breast and two slices cheese between the breads, with the cream cheese inside and the side with butter.

4. Place the sandwiches in the basket of the air fryer. Set the timer of the air fryer for 5 minutes and press the power button.

Nutrition: Calories: 294 Fat: 23g Carbs: 7g Proteins: 11g Sugar: 14g; Fiber: 12g; Sodium: 143mg

Dinner Recipes

71.   Cauliflower Mac & Cheese

Preparation Time: 5 Minutes

Cooking Time: 25 Minutes

Effort: Easy

Serving Size: 4

Ingredients:

- 1 Cauliflower Head, torn into florets
- Salt & Black Pepper, as needed
- ¼ cup Almond Milk, unsweetened
- ¼ cup Heavy Cream
- 3 tbsp. Butter, preferably grass-fed
- 1 cup Cheddar Cheese, shredded

Directions:

1. Preheat the oven to 450 F.

2. Melt the butter in a small microwave-safe bowl and heat it for 30 seconds.

3. Pour the melted butter over the cauliflower florets along with salt and pepper. Toss them well.

4. Place the cauliflower florets in a parchment paper-covered large baking sheet.

5. Bake them for 15 minutes or until the cauliflower is crisp-tender.

6. Once baked, mix the heavy cream, cheddar cheese, almond milk, and the remaining butter in a large microwave-safe bowl and heat it on high heat for 2 minutes or until the cheese mixture is smooth. Repeat the procedure until the cheese has melted.

7. Finally, stir in the cauliflower to the sauce mixture and coat well.

Nutrition: Calories: 294 Fat: 23g Carbs: 7g Proteins: 11g Sugar: 14g; Fiber: 12g; Sodium: 143mg

72.   Easy Egg Salad

Preparation Time: 5 Minutes

Cooking Time: 15 to 20 Minutes

Effort: Easy

Servings: 4

Ingredients:

- 6 Eggs, preferably free-range
- ¼ tsp. Salt
- 2 tbsp. Mayonnaise
- 1 tsp. Lemon juice
- 1 tsp. Dijon mustard

- Pepper, to taste

- Lettuce leaves, to serve

Directions:

1. Keep the eggs in a saucepan of water and pour cold water until it covers the egg by another 1 inch.

2. Bring to a boil and then remove the eggs from heat.

3. Peel the eggs under cold running water.

4. Transfer the cooked eggs into a food processor and pulse them until chopped.

5. Stir in the mayonnaise, lemon juice, salt, Dijon mustard, and pepper and mix them well.

6. Taste for seasoning and add more if required.

7. Serve in the lettuce leaves.

Nutrition: Calories: 166 Fat: 14g Carbs - 0.85g Proteins: 10g Sodium: 132mg Sugar: 14g; Fiber: 12g;

73.   Baked Chicken Legs

Preparation Time: 10 Minutes

Cooking Time: 40 Minutes

Effort: Easy

Servings: 6

Ingredients:

- 6 Chicken Legs

- ¼ tsp. Black Pepper

- ¼ cup Butter

- 1/2 tsp. Sea Salt

- 1/2 tsp. Smoked Paprika

- 1/2 tsp. Garlic Powder

Directions:

1. Preheat the oven to 425 F.

2. Pat the chicken legs with a paper towel to absorb any excess moisture.

3. Marinate the chicken pieces by first applying the butter over them and then with the seasoning. Set it aside for a few minutes.

4. Bake them for 25 minutes. Turnover and bake for further 10 minutes or until the internal temperature reaches 165 F.

5. Serve them hot.

Nutrition: Calories: 236 Fat16g Carbs: 0g Protein: 22g Sodium: 314mg Sugar: 10g; Fiber: 5g;

74.   Creamed Spinach

Preparation Time: 5 Minutes

Cooking Time: 10 Minutes

Effort: Easy

Servings: 4

Ingredients:

- 3 tbsp. Butter

- ¼ tsp. Black Pepper

- 4 cloves of Garlic, minced

- ¼ tsp. Sea Salt

- 10 oz. Baby Spinach, chopped

- 1 tsp. Italian Seasoning

- 1/2 cup Heavy Cream

- 3 oz. Cream Cheese

Directions:

1. Melt butter in a large sauté pan over medium heat.

2. Once the butter has melted, spoon in the garlic and sauté for 30 seconds or until aromatic.

3. Spoon in the spinach and cook for 3 to 4 minutes or until wilted.

4. Add all the remaining ingredients to it and continuously stir until the cream cheese melts and the mixture gets thickened.

5. Serve hot

Nutrition: Calories: 274 Fat27g Carbs: 4g Protein: 4g Sodium: 114mg Sugar: 10g; Fiber: 9g;

75.   Stuffed Mushrooms

Preparation Time: 10 Minutes

Cooking Time: 20 Minutes

Servings: 4

Ingredients:

- 4 Portobello Mushrooms, large

- 1/2 cup Mozzarella Cheese, shredded

- 1/2 cup Marinara, low-sugar

- Olive Oil Spray

Directions:

1. Preheat the oven to 375 F.

2. Take out the dark gills from the mushrooms with the help of a spoon.

3. Keep the mushroom stem upside down and spoon it with two tablespoons of marinara sauce and mozzarella cheese.

4. Bake for 18 minutes or until the cheese is bubbly.

Nutrition: Calories: 113 Fat6g Carbs: 4g Protein: 7g Sodium: 14mg Sugar: 11g; Fiber: 8g;

76.   Vegetable Soup

Preparation Time: 10 Minutes

Cooking Time: 30 Minutes

Servings: 5

Ingredients:

- 8 cups Vegetable Broth

- 2 tbsp. Olive Oil

- 1 tbsp. Italian Seasoning

- 1 Onion, large & diced

- 2 Bay Leaves, dried

- 2 Bell Pepper, large & diced

- Sea Salt & Black Pepper, as needed

- 4 cloves of Garlic, minced

- 28 oz. Tomatoes, diced

- 1 Cauliflower head, medium & torn into florets

- 2 cups Green Beans, trimmed & chopped

Directions:

1. Heat oil in a Dutch oven over medium heat.

2. Once the oil becomes hot, stir in the onions and pepper.

3. Cook for 10 minutes or until the onion is softened and browned.

4. Spoon in the garlic and sauté for a minute or until fragrant.

5. Add all the remaining ingredients to it. Mix until everything comes together.

6. Bring the mixture to a boil. Lower the heat and cook for further 20 minutes or until the vegetables have softened.

7. Serve hot.

Nutrition: Calories: 79 Fat 2g Carbs: 8g Protein: 2g Sugar: 14g; Fiber: 12g; Sodium: 143mg

77.   Pork Chop Diane

Preparation Time: 10 minutes

Cooking Time: 20 minutes

Serving: 4

Ingredients:

- ¼ cup low-sodium chicken broth

- 1 tablespoon freshly squeezed lemon juice

- 2 teaspoons Worcestershire sauce

- 2 teaspoons Dijon mustard

- 4 (5-ounce) boneless pork top loin chops

- 1 teaspoon extra-virgin olive oil

- 1 teaspoon lemon zest

- 1 teaspoon butter

- 2 teaspoons chopped fresh chives

Direction:

1. Blend together the chicken broth, lemon juice, Worcestershire sauce, and Dijon mustard and set it aside.

2. Season the pork chops lightly.

3. Situate large skillet over medium-high heat and add the olive oil.

4. Cook the pork chops, turning once, until they are no longer pink, about 8 minutes per side.

5. Put aside the chops.

6. Pour the broth mixture into the skillet and cook until warmed through and thickened, about 2 minutes.

7. Blend lemon zest, butter, and chives.

8. Garnish with a generous spoonful of sauce.

Nutrition: Calories 200 Fat 8g Carbs 1g Sugar: 12g; Fiber: 10g; Sodium: 138mg

78.   Autumn Pork Chops with Red Cabbage and Apples

Preparation Time: 15 minutes

Cooking Time: 30 minutes

Serving: 4

Ingredients:

- ¼ cup apple cider vinegar

- 2 tablespoons granulated sweetener

- 4 (4-ounce) pork chops, about 1 inch thick

- 1 tablespoon extra-virgin olive oil

- ½ red cabbage, finely shredded

- 1 sweet onion, thinly sliced

- 1 apple, peeled, cored, and sliced

- 1 teaspoon chopped fresh thyme

Direction:

67

1. Scourge together the vinegar and sweetener. Set it aside.

2. Season the pork with salt and pepper.

3. Position huge skillet over medium-high heat and add the olive oil.

4. Cook the pork chops until no longer pink, turning once, about 8 minutes per side.

5. Put chops aside.

6. Add the cabbage and onion to the skillet and sauté until the vegetables have softened, about 5 minutes.

7. Add the vinegar mixture and the apple slices to the skillet and bring the mixture to a boil.

8. Adjust heat to low and simmer, covered, for 5 additional minutes.

9. Return the pork chops to the skillet, along with any accumulated juices and thyme, cover, and cook for 5 more minutes.

Nutrition: Calories 223 Carbs 12g Fiber 3g Protein: 15g; Sugar: 11g; Sodium: 396mg

79.   Chipotle Chili Pork Chops

Preparation Time: 4 hours

Cooking Time: 20 minutes

Serving: 4

Ingredients:

- Juice and zest of 1 lime

- 1 tablespoon extra-virgin olive oil

- 1 tablespoon chipotle chili powder

- 2 teaspoons minced garlic

- 1 teaspoon ground cinnamon

- Pinch sea salt

- 4 (5-ounce) pork chops

Direction:

1. Combine the lime juice and zest, oil, chipotle chili powder, garlic, cinnamon, and salt in a resealable plastic bag. Add the pork chops. Remove as much air as possible and seal the bag.

2. Marinate the chops in the refrigerator for at least 4 hours, and up to 24 hours, turning them several times.

3. Ready the oven to 400°F and set a rack on a baking sheet. Let the chops rest at room temperature for 15 minutes, then arrange them on the rack and discard the remaining marinade.

4. Roast the chops until cooked through, turning once, about 10 minutes per side.

5. Serve with lime wedges.

Nutrition: Calories 204 Carbs 1g Sugar 1g Protein: 15g; Fiber: 11g; Sodium: 420mg

80.   Orange-Marinated Pork Tenderloin

Preparation Time: 2 hours

Cooking Time: 30 minutes

Serving: 4

Ingredients:

- ¼ cup freshly squeezed orange juice

- 2 teaspoons orange zest

- 2 teaspoons minced garlic

- 1 teaspoon low-sodium soy sauce

- 1 teaspoon grated fresh ginger

- 1 teaspoon honey

- 1½ pounds pork tenderloin roast

- 1 tablespoon extra-virgin olive oil

Direction:

1. Blend together the orange juice, zest, garlic, soy sauce, ginger, and honey.

2. Pour the marinade into a resealable plastic bag and add the pork tenderloin.

3. Remove as much air as possible and seal the bag. Marinate the pork in the refrigerator, turning the bag a few times, for 2 hours.

4. Preheat the oven to 400°F.

5. Pull out tenderloin from the marinade and discard the marinade.

6. Position big ovenproof skillet over medium-high heat and add the oil.

7. Sear the pork tenderloin on all sides, about 5 minutes in total.

8. Position skillet to the oven and roast for 25 minutes.

9. Put aside for 10 minutes before serving.

Nutrition: Calories 228 Carbs 4g Sugar 3g Protein: 15g; Fiber: 9g; Sodium: 345mg

81.   Homestyle Herb Meatballs

Preparation Time: 10 minutes

Cooking Time: 15 minutes

Serving: 4

Ingredients:

- ½ pound lean ground pork

- ½ pound lean ground beef

- 1 sweet onion, finely chopped

- ¼ cup bread crumbs

- 2 tablespoons chopped fresh basil

- 2 teaspoons minced garlic

- 1 egg

Direction:

1. Preheat the oven to 350°F.

2. Ready baking tray with parchment paper and set it aside.

3. In a large bowl, mix together the pork, beef, onion, bread crumbs, basil, garlic, egg, salt, and pepper until very well mixed.

4. Roll the meat mixture into 2-inch meatballs.

5. Transfer the meatballs to the baking sheet and bake until they are browned and cooked through, about 15 minutes.

6. Serve the meatballs with your favorite marinara sauce and some steamed green beans.

Nutrition: Calories 332 Carbs 13g Sugar 3g Protein: 15g; Carbs: 71g; Fiber: 9g; Sodium: 396mg

82.   Lime-Parsley Lamb Cutlets

Preparation Time: 4 hours

Cooking Time: 10 minutes

Serving: 4

Ingredients:

- ¼ cup extra-virgin olive oil

- ¼ cup freshly squeezed lime juice

- 2 tablespoons lime zest

- 2 tablespoons chopped fresh parsley

- 12 lamb cutlets (about 1½ pounds total)

Direction:

1. Scourge the oil, lime juice, zest, parsley, salt, and pepper.

2. Pour marinade to a resealable plastic bag.

3. Add the cutlets to the bag and remove as much air as possible before sealing.

4. Marinate the lamb in the refrigerator for about 4 hours, turning the bag several times.

5. Preheat the oven to broil.

6. Remove the chops from the bag and arrange them on an aluminum foil–lined baking sheet. Discard the marinade.

7. Broil the chops for 4 minutes per side for medium doneness.

8. Let the chops rest for 5 minutes before serving.

Nutrition: Calories 413 Carbs 31g Protein: 15g; Sugar: 11g; Fiber: 12g; Sodium: 228mg

83. Mediterranean Steak Sandwiches

Preparation Time: 1 hour

Cooking Time: 10 minutes

Serving: 4

Ingredients:

- 2 tablespoons extra-virgin olive oil

- 2 tablespoons balsamic vinegar

- 2 teaspoons garlic

- 2 teaspoons lemon juice

- 2 teaspoons fresh oregano

- 1 teaspoon fresh parsley

- 1-pound flank steak

- 4 whole-wheat pitas

- 2 cups shredded lettuce

- 1 red onion, thinly sliced

- 1 tomato, chopped

- 1 ounce low-sodium feta cheese

Direction:

1. Scourge olive oil, balsamic vinegar, garlic, lemon juice, oregano, and parsley.

2. Add the steak to the bowl, turning to coat it completely.

3. Marinate the steak for 1 hour in the refrigerator, turning it over several times.

4. Preheat the broiler. Line a baking sheet with aluminum foil.

5. Put steak out of the bowl and discard the marinade.

6. Situate steak on the baking sheet and broil for 5 minutes per side for medium.

7. Set aside for 10 minutes before slicing.

8. Stuff the pitas with the sliced steak, lettuce, onion, tomato, and feta.

Nutrition: Calories 344 Carbs 22g Fiber 3g Sodium: 396mg Protein: 15g; Carbs: 71g; Sugar: 11g;

84. Roasted Beef with Peppercorn Sauce

Preparation Time: 10 minutes

Cooking Time: 90 minutes

Serving: 4

Ingredients:

- 1½ pounds top rump beef roast
- 3 teaspoons extra-virgin olive oil
- 3 shallots, minced
- 2 teaspoons minced garlic
- 1 tablespoon green peppercorns
- 2 tablespoons dry sherry
- 2 tablespoons all-purpose flour
- 1 cup sodium-free beef broth

Direction:

1. Heat the oven to 300°F.
2. Season the roast with salt and pepper.
3. Position huge skillet over medium-high heat and add 2 teaspoons of olive oil.
4. Brown the beef on all sides, about 10 minutes in total, and transfer the roast to a baking dish.
5. Roast until desired doneness, about 1½ hours for medium. When the roast has been in the oven for 1 hour, start the sauce.
6. In a medium saucepan over medium-high heat, sauté the shallots in the remaining 1 teaspoon of olive oil until translucent, about 4 minutes.
7. Stir in the garlic and peppercorns, and cook for another minute. Whisk in the sherry to deglaze the pan.
8. Whisk in the flour to form a thick paste, cooking for 1 minute and stirring constantly.

9. Fill in the beef broth and whisk for 4 minutes. Season the sauce.
10. Serve the beef with a generous spoonful of sauce.

Nutrition: Calories 330 Carbs 4g Protein 36g Carbs: 71g; Sugar: 11g; Fiber: 9g; Sodium: 286mg

85.   Coffee-and-Herb-Marinated Steak

Preparation Time: 2 hours

Cooking Time: 10 minutes

Serving: 3

Ingredients:

- ¼ cup whole coffee beans
- 2 teaspoons garlic
- 2 teaspoons rosemary
- 2 teaspoons thyme
- 1 teaspoon black pepper
- 2 tablespoons apple cider vinegar
- 2 tablespoons extra-virgin olive oil
- 1-pound flank steak, trimmed of visible fat

Direction:

1. Place the coffee beans, garlic, rosemary, thyme, and black pepper in a coffee grinder or food processor and pulse until coarsely ground.
2. Transfer the coffee mixture to a resealable plastic bag and add the vinegar and oil. Shake to combine.
3. Add the flank steak and squeeze the excess air out of the bag. Seal it. Marinate the steak in the refrigerator for at least 2 hours, occasionally turning the bag over.

4. Preheat the broiler. Line a baking sheet with aluminum foil.

5. Pull the steak out and discard the marinade.

6. Position steak on the baking sheet and broil until it is done to your liking.

7. Put aside for 10 minutes before cutting it.

8. Serve with your favorite side dish.

Nutrition: Calories 313 Fat 31g Protein 20g Carbs: 68g; Sugar: 9g; Fiber: 9g; Sodium: 277mg

86.   Traditional Beef Stroganoff

Preparation Time: 10 minutes

Cooking Time: 30 minutes

Serving: 4

Ingredients:

- 1 teaspoon extra-virgin olive oil

- 1-pound top sirloin, cut into thin strips

- 1 cup sliced button mushrooms

- ½ sweet onion, finely chopped

- 1 teaspoon minced garlic

- 1 tablespoon whole-wheat flour

- ½ cup low-sodium beef broth

- ¼ cup dry sherry

- ½ cup fat-free sour cream

- 1 tablespoon chopped fresh parsley

Direction:

1. Position the skillet over medium-high heat and add the oil.

2. Sauté the beef until browned, about 10 minutes, then remove the beef with a slotted spoon to a plate and set it aside.

3. Add the mushrooms, onion, and garlic to the skillet and sauté until lightly browned, about 5 minutes.

4. Whisk in the flour and then whisk in the beef broth and sherry.

5. Return the sirloin to the skillet and bring the mixture to a boil.

6. Reduce the heat to low and simmer until the beef is tender, about 10 minutes.

7. Stir in the sour cream and parsley. Season with salt and pepper.

Nutrition: Calories 257 Carbs 6g Fiber 1g Protein: 15g; Sugar: 11g; Sodium: 346mg

87.   Chicken and Roasted Vegetable Wraps

Preparation Time: 10 minutes

Cooking Time: 20 minutes

Serving: 4

Ingredients:

- ½ small eggplant

- 1 red bell pepper

- 1 medium zucchini

- ½ small red onion, sliced

- 1 tablespoon extra-virgin olive oil

- 2 (8-ounce) cooked chicken breasts, sliced

- 4 whole-wheat tortilla wraps

Direction:

1. Preheat the oven to 400°F.

2. Wrap baking sheet with foil and set it aside.

3. In a large bowl, toss the eggplant, bell pepper, zucchini, and red onion with the olive oil.

4. Transfer the vegetables to the baking sheet and lightly season with salt and pepper.

5. Roast the vegetables until soft and slightly charred, about 20 minutes.

6. Divide the vegetables and chicken into four portions.

7. Wrap 1 tortilla around each portion of chicken and grilled vegetables, and serve.

Nutrition: Calories 483 Carbs 45g Fiber 3g Sodium: 396mg Protein: 15g; Sugar: 11g;

88.   Spicy Chicken Cacciatore

Preparation Time: 20 minutes

Cooking Time: 1 hour

Serving: 6

Ingredients:

- 1 (2-pound) chicken

- ¼ cup all-purpose flour

- 2 tablespoons extra-virgin olive oil

- 3 slices bacon

- 1 sweet onion

- 2 teaspoons minced garlic

- 4 ounces button mushrooms, halved

- 1 (28-ounce) can low-sodium stewed tomatoes

- ½ cup red wine

- 2 teaspoons chopped fresh oregano

Direction:

1. Cut the chicken into pieces: 2 drumsticks, 2 thighs, 2 wings, and 4 breast pieces.

2. Dredge the chicken pieces in the flour and season each piece with salt and pepper.

3. Place a large skillet over medium-high heat and add the olive oil.

4. Brown the chicken pieces on all sides, about 20 minutes in total. Transfer the chicken to a plate.

5. Cook chopped bacon to the skillet for 5 minutes. With a slotted spoon, transfer the cooked bacon to the same plate as the chicken.

6. Pour off most of the oil from the skillet, leaving just a light coating. Sauté the onion, garlic, and mushrooms in the skillet until tender, about 4 minutes.

7. Stir in the tomatoes, wine, oregano, and red pepper flakes.

8. Bring the sauce to a boil. Return the chicken and bacon, plus any accumulated juices from the plate, to the skillet.

9. Reduce the heat to low and simmer until the chicken is tender, about 30 minutes.

Nutrition: Calories 230 Carbs 14g Fiber 2g Protein: 15g; Sugar: 11g; Sodium: 327mg

89.   Scallion Sandwich

Preparation Time: 10 minutes

Cooking Time: 10 minutes

Servings: 1

Ingredients:

- 2 slices wheat bread

- 2 teaspoons butter, low fat

- 2 scallions, sliced thinly

- 1 tablespoon of parmesan cheese, grated

- 3/4 cup of cheddar cheese, reduced fat, grated

Directions:

1. Preheat the Air fryer to 356 degrees.

2. Spread butter on a slice of bread. Place inside the cooking basket with the butter side facing down.

3. Place cheese and scallions on top. Spread the rest of the butter on the other slice of bread Put it on top of the sandwich and sprinkle with parmesan cheese.

4. Cook for 10 minutes.

Nutrition: Calorie: 154 Carbs: 9g Fat: 2.5g Protein: 8.6g Fiber: 2.4g Protein: 15g; Sugar: 21g; Sodium: 276mg

90. Lean Lamb and Turkey Meatballs with Yogurt

Preparation Time: 10 minutes

Servings: 4

Cooking Time: 8 minutes

Ingredients:

- 1 egg white

- 4 ounces ground lean turkey

- 1 pound of ground lean lamb

- 1 teaspoon each of cayenne pepper, ground coriander, red chili pastes, salt, and ground cumin

- 2 garlic cloves, minced

- 1 1/2 tablespoons parsley, chopped

- 1 tablespoon mint, chopped

- 1/4 cup of olive oil

For the yogurt

- 2 tablespoons of buttermilk

- 1 garlic clove, minced

- 1/4 cup mint, chopped

- 1/2 cup of Greek yogurt, non-fat

- Salt to taste

Directions:

1. Set the Air Fryer to 390 degrees.

2. Mix all the ingredients for the meatballs in a bowl. Roll and mold them into golf-size round pieces. Arrange in the cooking basket. Cook for 8 minutes.

3. While waiting, combine all the ingredients for the mint yogurt in a bowl. Mix well.

4. Serve the meatballs with the mint yogurt. Top with olives and fresh mint.

Nutrition: Calorie: 154 Carbohydrate: 9g Fat: 2.5g Protein: 8.6g Fiber: 2.4g

91. Air Fried Section and Tomato

Preparation Time: 10 minutes

Cooking Time: 5 minutes

Servings: 2

Ingredients:

- 1 aubergine, sliced thickly into 4 disks

- 1 tomato, sliced into 2 thick disks

- 2 tsp. feta cheese, reduced fat

- 2 fresh basil leaves, minced

- 2 balls, small buffalo mozzarella, reduced fat, roughly torn

- Pinch of salt

- Pinch of black pepper

Directions:

1. Preheat Air Fryer to 330 degrees F.

2. Spray small amount of oil into the Air fryer basket. Fry aubergine slices for 5 minutes or until golden brown on both sides. Transfer to a plate.

3. Fry tomato slices in batches for 5 minutes or until seared on both sides.

4. To serve, stack salad starting with an aborigine base, buffalo mozzarella, basil leaves, tomato slice, and 1/2-teaspoon feta cheese.

5. Top of with another slice of aborigine and 1/2 tsp. feta cheese. Serve.

Nutrition: Calorie: 140.3 Carbs: 26.6 Fat: 3.4g Protein: 4.2g Fiber: 7.3g Sugar: 11g; Sodium: 343mg

92. Cheesy Salmon Fillets

Preparation Time: 15 minutes

Cooking Time: 20 minutes

Servings: 2-3

Ingredients:

For the salmon fillets

- 2 pieces, 4 oz. each salmon fillets, choose even cuts

- 1/2 cup sour cream, reduced fat

- ¼ cup cottage cheese, reduced fat

- ¼ cup Parmigiano-Reggiano cheese, freshly grated

Garnish:

- Spanish paprika

- 1/2 piece lemon, cut into wedges

Directions:

1. Preheat Air Fryer to 330 degrees F.

2. To make the salmon fillets, mix sour cream, cottage cheese, and Parmigiano-Reggiano cheese in a bowl.

3. Layer salmon fillets in the Air fryer basket. Fry for 20 minutes or until cheese turns golden brown.

4. To assemble, place a salmon fillet and sprinkle paprika. Garnish with lemon wedges and squeeze lemon juice on top. Serve.

Nutrition: Calorie: 274 Carbs: 1g Fat: 19g Protein: 24g Fiber: 0.5g Sugar: 11g; Sodium: 368mg

93. Salmon with Asparagus

Preparation Time: 5 Minutes

Cooking Time: 10 Minutes

Servings: 3

Ingredients:

- 1 lb. Salmon, sliced into fillets

- 1 tbsp. Olive Oil

- Salt & Pepper, as needed

- 1 bunch of Asparagus, trimmed

- 2 cloves of Garlic, minced

- Zest & Juice of 1/2 Lemon
- 1 tbsp. Butter, salted

Directions:

1. Spoon in the butter and olive oil into a large pan and heat it over medium-high heat.

2. Once it becomes hot, place the salmon and season it with salt and pepper.

3. Cook for 4 minutes per side and then cook the other side.

4. Stir in the garlic and lemon zest to it.

5. Cook for further 2 minutes or until slightly browned.

6. Off the heat and squeeze the lemon juice over it.

7. Serve it hot.

Nutrition: Calories: 409 Carbs: 2.7g Proteins: 32.8g Fat: 28.8g Sugar: 11g; Fiber: 9g; Sodium: 497mg

94.   Shrimp in Garlic Butter

Preparation Time: 5 Minutes

Cooking Time: 20 Minutes

Servings: 4

Ingredients:

- 1 lb. Shrimp, peeled & deveined
- ¼ tsp. Red Pepper Flakes
- 6 tbsp. Butter, divided
- 1/2 cup Chicken Stock
- Salt & Pepper, as needed

- 2 tbsp. Parsley, minced
- 5 cloves of Garlic, minced
- 2 tbsp. Lemon Juice

Directions:

1. Heat a large bottomed skillet over medium-high heat.

2. Spoon in two tablespoons of the butter and melt it. Add the shrimp.

3. Season it with salt and pepper. Sear for 4 minutes or until shrimp gets cooked.

4. Transfer the shrimp to a plate and stir in the garlic.

5. Sauté for 30 seconds or until aromatic.

6. Pour the chicken stock and whisk it well. Allow it to simmer for 5 to 10 minutes or until it has reduced to half.

7. Spoon the remaining butter, red pepper, and lemon juice to the sauce. Mix.

8. Continue cooking for another 2 minutes.

9. Take off the pan from the heat and add the cooked shrimp to it.

10. Garnish with parsley and transfer to the serving bowl.

11. Enjoy.

Nutrition: Calories: 307 Carbs: 3g Proteins: 27g Fat: 20g Sugar: 14g; Fiber: 7g; Sodium: 522mg

95.   Cobb Salad

Keto & Under 30 Minutes

Preparation Time: 5 Minutes

Cooking Time: 5 Minutes

Servings: 1

Ingredients:

- 4 Cherry Tomatoes, chopped
- ¼ cup Bacon, cooked & crumbled
- 1/2 of 1 Avocado, chopped
- 2 oz. Chicken Breast, shredded
- 1 Egg, hardboiled
- 2 cups Mixed Green salad
- 1 oz. Feta Cheese, crumbled

Directions:

1. Toss all the ingredients for the Cobb salad in a large mixing bowl and toss well.
2. Serve and enjoy it.

Nutrition: Calories: 307 Carbs: 3g Proteins: 27g Fat: 20g Sugar: 11g; Fiber: 11g; Sodium: 522mg

96.   Beef Chili

Preparation Time: 10 Minutes

Cooking Time: 20 Minutes

Serving Size: 4

Ingredients:

- 1/2 tsp. Garlic Powder
- 1 tsp. Coriander, grounded
- 1 lb. Beef, grounded
- 1/2 tsp. Sea Salt
- 1/2 tsp. Cayenne Pepper
- 1 tsp. Cumin, grounded
- 1/2 tsp. Pepper, grounded
- 1/2 cup Salsa, low-carb & no-sugar

Directions:

1. Heat a large-sized pan over medium-high heat and cook the beef in it until browned.
2. Stir in all the spices and cook them for 7 minutes or until everything is combined.
3. When the beef gets cooked, spoon in the salsa.
4. Bring the mixture to a simmer and cook for another 8 minutes or until everything comes together.
5. Take it from heat and transfer to a serving bowl.

Nutrition: Calories: 229 Fat: 10g Carbs: 2g Proteins: 33g Sugar: 11g; Fiber: 9g; Sodium: 675mg

97.   Greek Broccoli Salad

Preparation Time: 10 Minutes

Cooking Time: 15 Minutes

Servings: 4

Ingredients:

- 1 ¼ lb. Broccoli, sliced into small bites
- ¼ cup Almonds, sliced
- 1/3 cup Sun-dried Tomatoes
- ¼ cup Feta Cheese, crumbled
- ¼ cup Red Onion, sliced

For the dressing:

- 1/4 cup Olive Oil
- Dash of Red Pepper Flakes
- 1 Garlic clove, minced

- ¼ tsp. Salt
- 2 tbsp. Lemon Juice
- 1/2 tsp. Dijon Mustard
- 1 tsp. Low Carb Sweetener Syrup
- 1/2 tsp. Oregano, dried

Directions:

1. Mix broccoli, onion, almonds and sun-dried tomatoes in a large mixing bowl.

2. In another small-sized bowl, combine all the dressing ingredients until emulsified.

3. Spoon the dressing over the broccoli salad.

4. Allow the salad to rest for half an hour before serving.

Nutrition: Calories: 272 Carbs: 11.9g Proteins: 8g Fat: 21.6g Sugar: 11g; Fiber: 9g; Sodium: 321mg

98.   Cheesy Cauliflower Gratin

Preparation Time: 5 Minutes

Cooking Time: 25 Minutes

Servings: 6

Ingredients:

- 6 deli slices Pepper Jack Cheese
- 4 cups Cauliflower florets
- Salt and Pepper, as needed
- 4 tbsp. Butter
- 1/3 cup Heavy Whipping Cream

Directions:

1. Mix the cauliflower, cream, butter, salt, and pepper in a safe microwave bowl and combine well.

2. Microwave the cauliflower mixture for 25 minutes on high until it becomes soft and tender.

3. Remove the ingredients from the bowl and mash with the help of a fork.

4. Taste for seasonings and spoon in salt and pepper as required.

5. Arrange the slices of pepper jack cheese on top of the cauliflower mixture and microwave for 3 minutes until the cheese starts melting.

6. Serve warm.

Nutrition: Calories: 421 Carbs: 3g Proteins: 19g Fat: 37g Sugar: 11g; Fiber: 11g; Sodium: 111mg

99.   Strawberry Spinach Salad

Preparation Time: 5 Minutes

Cooking Time: 10 Minutes

Servings: 4

Ingredients:

- 4 oz. Feta Cheese, crumbled
- 8 Strawberries, sliced
- 2 oz. Almonds
- 6 Slices Bacon, thick-cut, crispy and crumbled
- 10 oz. Spinach leaves, fresh
- 2 Roma Tomatoes, diced
- 2 oz. Red Onion, sliced thinly

Directions:

1. For making this healthy salad, mix all the ingredients needed to make the salad in a large-sized bowl and toss them well.

Nutrition: Calories: 255kcal Fat: 16g Carbohydrates: 8g Proteins: 14g Sodium: 27mg

100. Garlic Bread

Preparation time: 10 minutes

Cooking time: 15 minutes

Servings: 4-5

Ingredients:

- 2 stale French rolls

- 4 tbsp. crushed or crumpled garlic

- 1 cup of mayonnaise

- Powdered grated Parmesan

- 1 tbsp. olive oil

Directions:

1. Preheat the air fryer. Set the time of 5 minutes and the temperature to 2000C.

2. Mix mayonnaise with garlic and set aside.

3. Cut the baguettes into slices, but without separating them completely.

4. Fill the cavities of equals. Brush with olive oil and sprinkle with grated cheese.

5. Place in the basket of the air fryer. Set the timer to 10 minutes, adjust the temperature to 1800C and press the power button.

Nutrition: Calories: 340 Fat: 15g Carbs: 32g Protein: 15g Sugar: 0g Fiber: 9g; Sodium: 396mg

101. Bruschetta

Preparation time: 5 minutes

Cooking time: 10 minutes

Servings: 2

Ingredients:

- 4 slices of Italian bread

- 1 cup chopped tomato tea

- 1 cup grated mozzarella tea

- Olive oil

- Oregano, salt, and pepper

- 4 fresh basil leaves

Directions:

1. Preheat the air fryer. Set the timer of 5 minutes and the temperature to 2000C.

2. Sprinkle the slices of Italian bread with olive oil. Divide the chopped tomatoes and mozzarella between the slices. Season with salt, pepper, and oregano.

3. Put oil in the filling. Place a basil leaf on top of each slice.

4. Put the bruschetta in the basket of the air fryer being careful not to spill the filling. Set the timer of 5 minutes, set the temperature to 180C, and press the power button.

5. Transfer the bruschetta to a plate and serve.

Nutrition: Calories: 434 Fat: 14g Carbs: 63g Protein: 11g Sugar: 8g Fiber: 9g; Sodium: 276mg

102. Cream Buns with Strawberries

Preparation time: 10 minutes

Cooking time: 12 minutes

Servings: 6

Ingredients:

- 240g all-purpose flour
- 50g granulated sugar
- 8g baking powder
- 1g of salt
- 85g chopped cold butter
- 84g chopped fresh strawberries
- 120 ml whipping cream
- 2 large eggs
- 10 ml vanilla extract
- 5 ml of water

Directions:

1. Sift flour, sugar, baking powder and salt in a large bowl. Put the butter with the flour with the use of a blender or your hands until the mixture resembles thick crumbs.

2. Mix the strawberries in the flour mixture. Set aside for the mixture to stand. Beat the whipping cream, 1 egg and the vanilla extract in a separate bowl.

3. Put the cream mixture in the flour mixture until they are homogeneous, and then spread the mixture to a thickness of 38 mm.

4. Use a round cookie cutter to cut the buns. Spread the buns with a combination of egg and water. Set aside

5. Preheat the air fryer, set it to 180C.

6. Place baking paper in the preheated inner basket.

7. Place the buns on top of the baking paper and cook for 12 minutes at 180C, until golden brown.

Nutrition: Calories: 150Fat: 14g Carbs: 3g Protein: 11g Sugar: 8g Fiber: 12g; Sodium: 396mg

103.   Blueberry Buns

Preparation time: 10 minutes

Cooking time: 12 minutes

Servings: 6

Ingredients:

- 240g all-purpose flour
- 50g granulated sugar
- 8g baking powder
- 2g of salt
- 85g chopped cold butter
- 85g of fresh blueberries
- 3g grated fresh ginger
- 113 ml whipping cream
- 2 large eggs
- 4 ml vanilla extract
- 5 ml of water

Directions:

1. Put sugar, flour, baking powder and salt in a large bowl.

2. Put the butter with the flour using a blender or your hands until the mixture resembles thick crumbs.

3. Mix the blueberries and ginger in the flour mixture and set aside

4. Mix the whipping cream, 1 egg and the vanilla extract in a different container.

5. Put the cream mixture with the flour mixture until combined.

6. Shape the dough until it reaches a thickness of approximately 38 mm and cut it into eighths.

7. Spread the buns with a combination of egg and water. Set aside Preheat the air fryer set it to 180C.

8. Place baking paper in the preheated inner basket and place the buns on top of the paper. Cook for 12 minutes at 180C, until golden brown

Nutrition: Calories: 105 Fat: 1.64g Carbs: 20.09g Protein: 2.43g Sugar: 2.1g Fiber: 9g; Sodium: 344mg

104. Cauliflower Potato Mash

Preparation Time: 30 minutes Servings: 4

Cooking Time: 5 minutes

Ingredients:

- 2 cups potatoes, peeled and cubed
- 2 tbsp. butter
- ¼ cup milk
- 10 oz. cauliflower florets
- ¾ tsp. salt

Directions:

1. Add water to the saucepan and bring to boil.

2. Reduce heat and simmer for 10 minutes.

3. Drain vegetables well. Transfer vegetables, butter, milk, and salt in a blender and blend until smooth.

4. Serve and enjoy.

Nutrition: Calories 128 Fat 6.2 g, Sugar 3.3 g, Protein 3.2 g, Fiber: 9g; Sodium: 354mg

Meat & Chicken Recipes

105. Roasted Pork & Apples

Preparation Time: 15 minutes

Cooking Time: 30 minutes

Servings: 4

Ingredients:

- Salt and pepper to taste
- 1/2 teaspoon dried, crushed
- 1 lb. pork tenderloin
- 1 tablespoon canola oil
- 1 onion, sliced into wedges
- 3 cooking apples, sliced into wedges
- 2/3 cup apple cider
- Sprigs fresh sage

Directions:

1. In a bowl, mix salt, pepper and sage.

2. Season both sides of pork with this mixture.

3. Place a pan over medium heat.

4. Brown both sides.

5. Transfer to a roasting pan.

6. Add the onion on top and around the pork.

7. Drizzle oil on top of the pork and apples.

8. Roast in the oven at 425 degrees F for 10 minutes.

9. Add the apples, roast for another 15 minutes.

10. In a pan, boil the apple cider and then simmer for 10 minutes.

11. Pour the apple cider sauce over the pork before serving.

Nutrition: Calories 239 Fat 6 g Sodium 209 mg Carbs 22 g Fiber 3 g Sugars 16 g Protein 24 g

106. Pork with Cranberry Relish

Preparation Time: 30 minutes

Cooking Time: 30 minutes

Servings: 4

Ingredients:

- 12 oz. pork tenderloin, fat trimmed and sliced crosswise

- Salt and pepper to taste

- ¼ cup all-purpose flour

- 2 tablespoons olive oil

- 1 onion, sliced thinly

- ¼ cup dried cranberries

- ¼ cup low-sodium chicken broth

- 1 tablespoon balsamic vinegar

Directions:

1. Flatten each slice of pork using a mallet.

2. In a dish, mix the salt, pepper and flour.

3. Dip each pork slice into the flour mixture.

4. Add oil to a pan over medium high heat.

5. Cook pork for 3 minutes per side or until golden crispy.

6. Transfer to a serving plate and cover with foil.

7. Cook the onion in the pan for 4 minutes.

8. Stir in the rest of the ingredients.

9. Simmer until the sauce has thickened.

Nutrition: Calories 211 Fat 9 g Sodium 116 mg Carbs 15 g Fiber 1 g Sugars 6 g Protein 18 g Potassium 378 mg

107. Sesame Pork with Mustard Sauce

Preparation Time: 25 minutes

Cooking Time: 25 minutes

Servings: 4

Ingredients:

- 2 tablespoons low-sodium teriyaki sauce

- ¼ cup chili sauce

- 2 cloves garlic, minced

- 2 teaspoons ginger, grated

- 2 pork tenderloins

- 2 teaspoons sesame seeds

- ¼ cup low fat sour cream

- 1 teaspoon Dijon mustard

- Salt to taste

- 1 scallion, chopped

Directions:

1. Preheat your oven to 425 degrees F.

2. Mix the teriyaki sauce, chili sauce, garlic and ginger.

3. Put the pork on a roasting pan.

4. Brush the sauce on both sides of the pork.

5. Bake in the oven for 15 minutes.

6. Brush with more sauce.

7. Top with sesame seeds.

8. Roast for 10 more minutes.

9. Mix the rest of the ingredients.

10. Serve the pork with mustard sauce.

Nutrition: Calories 135 Fat 3 g Carbs 7 g Fiber 1 g Sugars 15 g Protein 20 g Sodium 255 mg

108. Steak with Mushroom Sauce

Preparation Time: 20 minutes

Cooking Time: 5 minutes

Servings: 4

Ingredients:

- 12 oz. sirloin steak, sliced and trimmed

- 2 teaspoons grilling seasoning

- 2 teaspoons oil

- 6 oz. broccoli, trimmed

- 2 cups frozen peas

- 3 cups fresh mushrooms, sliced

- 1 cup beef broth (unsalted)

- 1 tablespoon mustard

- 2 teaspoons cornstarch

- Salt to taste

Directions:

1. Preheat your oven to 350 degrees F.

2. Season meat with grilling seasoning.

3. In a pan over medium high heat, cook the meat and broccoli for 4 minutes.

4. Sprinkle the peas around the steak.

5. Put the pan inside the oven and bake for 8 minutes.

6. Remove both meat and vegetables from the pan.

7. Add the mushrooms to the pan.

8. Cook for 3 minutes.

9. Mix the broth, mustard, salt and cornstarch.

10. Add to the mushrooms.

11. Cook for 1 minute.

12. Pour sauce over meat and vegetables before serving.

Nutrition: Calories 226 Fat 6 g Sodium 356 mg Carbs 16 g Fiber 5 g Sugars 6 g Protein 26 g

109. Steak with Tomato & Herbs

Preparation Time: 30 minutes

Cooking Time: 30 minutes

Servings: 2

Ingredients:

- 8 oz. beef loin steak, sliced in half

- Salt and pepper to taste

- Cooking spray

- 1 teaspoon fresh basil, snipped

- ¼ cup green onion, sliced

- 1/2 cup tomato, chopped

Directions:

1. Season the steak with salt and pepper.

2. Spray oil on your pan.

3. Put the pan over medium high heat.

4. Once hot, add the steaks.

5. Reduce heat to medium.

6. Cook for 10 to 13 minutes for medium, turning once.

7. Add the basil and green onion.

8. Cook for 2 minutes.

9. Add the tomato.

10. Cook for 1 minute.

11. Let cool a little before slicing.

Nutrition: Calories 170 Fat 6 g Sodium 207 mg Carbs 3 g Fiber 1 g Sugars 5 g Protein 25 g

110.   Barbecue Beef Brisket

Preparation Time: 25 minutes

Cooking Time: 10 hours

Servings: 10

Ingredients:

- 4 lb. beef brisket (boneless), trimmed and sliced

- 1 bay leaf

- 2 onions, sliced into rings

- 1/2 teaspoon dried thyme, crushed

- ¼ cup chili sauce

- 1 clove garlic, minced

- Salt and pepper to taste

- 2 tablespoons light brown sugar

- 2 tablespoons cornstarch

- 2 tablespoons cold water

Directions:

1. Put the meat in a slow cooker.

2. Add the bay leaf and onion.

3. In a bowl, mix the thyme, chili sauce, salt, pepper and sugar.

4. Pour the sauce over the meat.

5. Mix well.

6. Seal the pot and cook on low heat for 10 hours.

7. Discard the bay leaf.

8. Pour cooking liquid in a pan.

9. Add the mixed water and cornstarch.

10. Simmer until the sauce has thickened.

11. Pour the sauce over the meat.

Nutrition: Calories 182 Fat 6 g Sodium 217 mg Sugars 4 g Protein 20 g Potassium 383 mg

111.   Beef & Asparagus

Preparation Time: 15 minutes

Cooking Time: 10 minutes

Servings: 4

Ingredients:

- 2 teaspoons olive oil

- 1 lb. lean beef sirloin, trimmed and sliced

- 1 carrot, shredded

- Salt and pepper to taste

- 12 oz. asparagus, trimmed and sliced

- 1 teaspoon dried herbes de Provence, crushed

- 1/2 cup Marsala

- ¼ teaspoon lemon zest

Directions:

1. Pour oil in a pan over medium heat.

2. Add the beef and carrot.

3. Season with salt and pepper.

4. Cook for 3 minutes.

5. Add the asparagus and herbs.

6. Cook for 2 minutes.

7. Add the Marsala and lemon zest.

8. Cook for 5 minutes, stirring frequently.

Nutrition: Calories 327 Fat 7 g Sodium 209 mg Carbs 29 g Fiber 2 g Sugars 3 g Protein 28 g

112. Pork Chops with Grape Sauce

Preparation Time: 15 minutes

Cooking Time: 25 minutes

Servings: 4

Ingredients:

- Cooking spray

- 4 pork chops

- ¼ cup onion, sliced

- 1 clove garlic, minced

- 1/2 cup low-sodium chicken broth

- ¾ cup apple juice

- 1 tablespoon cornstarch

- 1 tablespoon balsamic vinegar

- 1 teaspoon honey

- 1 cup seedless red grapes, sliced in half

Directions:

1. Spray oil on your pan.

2. Put it over medium heat.

3. Add the pork chops to the pan.

4. Cook for 5 minutes per side.

5. Remove and set aside.

6. Add onion and garlic.

7. Cook for 2 minutes.

8. Pour in the broth and apple juice.

9. Bring to a boil.

10. Reduce heat to simmer.

11. Put the pork chops back to the skillet.

12. Simmer for 4 minutes.

13. In a bowl, mix the cornstarch, vinegar and honey.

14. Add to the pan.

15. Cook until the sauce has thickened.

16. Add the grapes.

17. Pour sauce over the pork chops before serving.

Nutrition: Calories 188 Fat 4 g Sodium 117 mg Carbs 18 g Fiber 1 g Sugars 13 g Protein 19 g

113. Italian Beef

Preparation Time: 20 minutes

Cooking Time: 1 hour and 20 minutes

Servings: 4

Ingredients:

- Cooking spray
- 1 lb. beef round steak, trimmed and sliced
- 1 cup onion, chopped
- 2 cloves garlic, minced
- 1 cup green bell pepper, chopped
- 1/2 cup celery, chopped
- 2 cups mushrooms, sliced
- 14 1/2 oz. canned diced tomatoes
- 1/2 teaspoon dried basil
- ¼ teaspoon dried oregano
- 1/8 teaspoon crushed red pepper
- 2 tablespoons Parmesan cheese, grated

Directions:

1. Spray oil on the pan over medium heat.
2. Cook the meat until brown on both sides.
3. Transfer meat to a plate.
4. Add the onion, garlic, bell pepper, celery and mushroom to the pan.
5. Cook until tender.
6. Add the tomatoes, herbs, and pepper.
7. Put the meat back to the pan.
8. Simmer while covered for 1 hour and 15 minutes.
9. Stir occasionally.
10. Sprinkle Parmesan cheese on top of the dish before serving.

Nutrition: Calories 212 Fat 4 g Sodium 296 mg Sugars 6 g Protein 30 g Potassium 876 mg

114. Lamb with Broccoli & Carrots

Preparation Time: 20 minutes

Cooking Time: 10 minutes

Servings: 4

Ingredients:

- 2 cloves garlic, minced
- 1 tablespoon fresh ginger, grated
- ¼ teaspoon red pepper, crushed
- 2 tablespoons low-sodium soy sauce
- 1 tablespoon white vinegar
- 1 tablespoon cornstarch
- 12 oz. lamb meat, trimmed and sliced
- 2 teaspoons cooking oil
- 1 lb. broccoli, sliced into florets
- 2 carrots, sliced into strips
- ¾ cup low-sodium beef broth
- 4 green onions, chopped
- 2 cups cooked spaghetti squash pasta

Directions:

1. Combine the garlic, ginger, red pepper, soy sauce, vinegar and cornstarch in a bowl.

2. Add lamb to the marinade.

3. Marinate for 10 minutes.

4. Discard marinade.

5. In a pan over medium heat, add the oil.

6. Add the lamb and cook for 3 minutes.

7. Transfer lamb to a plate.

8. Add the broccoli and carrots.

9. Cook for 1 minute.

10. Pour in the beef broth.

11. Cook for 5 minutes.

12. Put the meat back to the pan.

13. Sprinkle with green onion and serve on top of spaghetti squash.

Nutrition: Calories 205 Fat 6 g Sodium 659 mg Carbohydrate 17 g

115. Rosemary Lamb

Preparation Time: 15 minutes

Cooking Time: 2 hours

Servings: 14

Ingredients:

- Salt and pepper to taste

- 2 teaspoons fresh rosemary, snipped

- 5 lb. whole leg of lamb, trimmed and cut with slits on all sides

- 3 cloves garlic, slivered

- 1 cup water

Directions:

1. Preheat your oven to 375 degrees F.

2. Mix salt, pepper and rosemary in a bowl.

3. Sprinkle mixture all over the lamb.

4. Insert slivers of garlic into the slits.

5. Put the lamb on a roasting pan.

6. Add water to the pan.

7. Roast for 2 hours.

Nutrition: Calories 136 Fat 4 g Sodium 218 mg Protein 23 g Potassium 248 mg

116. Mediterranean Lamb Meatballs

Preparation Time: 10 minutes

Cooking Time: 20 minutes

Servings: 8

Ingredients:

- 12 oz. roasted red peppers

- 1 1/2 cups whole wheat breadcrumbs

- 2 eggs, beaten

- 1/3 cup tomato sauce

- 1/2 cup fresh basil

- ¼ cup parsley, snipped

- Salt and pepper to taste

- 2 lb. lean ground lamb

Directions:

1. Preheat your oven to 350 degrees F.

2. In a bowl, mix all the ingredients and then form into meatballs.

3. Put the meatballs on a baking pan.

4. Bake in the oven for 20 minutes.

Nutrition: Calories 94 Fat 3 g Sodium 170 mg Total Carbohydrate 2 g Fiber 1 g Sugars 0 g

117. Beef and Red Bean Chili

Preparation Time: 10 minutes

Cooking Time: 6 hours

Serving: 4

Ingredients

- 1 cup dry red beans
- 1 tablespoon olive oil
- 2 pounds boneless beef chuck
- 1 large onion, coarsely chopped
- 1 (14 ounce) can beef broth
- 2 chipotle chili peppers in adobo sauce
- 2 teaspoons dried oregano, crushed
- 1 teaspoon ground cumin
- ½ teaspoon salt
- 1 (14.5 ounce) can tomatoes with mild green chilis
- 1 (15 ounce) can tomato sauce
- ¼ cup snipped fresh cilantro
- 1 medium red sweet pepper

Direction

1. Rinse out the beans and place them into a Dutch oven or big saucepan, then add in water enough to cover them. Allow the beans to boil then drop the heat down. Simmer the beans without a cover for 10 minutes. Take off the heat and keep covered for an hour.

2. In a big frypan, heat up the oil upon medium-high heat, then cook onion and half the beef until they brown a bit over medium-high heat. Move into a 3 1/2- or 4-quart crockery cooker. Do this again with what's left of the beef. Add in tomato sauce, tomatoes (not drained), salt, cumin, oregano, adobo sauce, chipotle peppers, and broth, stirring to blend. Strain out and rinse beans and stir in the cooker.

3. Cook while covered on a low setting for around 10-12 hours or on high setting for 5-6 hours. Spoon the chili into bowls or mugs and top with sweet pepper and cilantro.

Nutrition: Calories 288 Carbs 24g Sugar 5g Protein: 15g; Fiber: 9g; Sodium: 396mg

118. Berry Apple Cider

Preparation Time: 15 minutes

Cooking Time: 3 hours

Serving: 3

Ingredients

- 4 cinnamon sticks, cut into 1-inch pieces
- 1½ teaspoons whole cloves
- 4 cups apple cider
- 4 cups low-calorie cranberry-raspberry juice drink
- 1 medium apple

Direction

1. To make the spice bag, cut out a 6-inch square from double thick, pure cotton cheesecloth. Put in the cloves and cinnamon, then bring the corners up, tie it closed using a clean kitchen string that is pure cotton.

2. In a 3 1/2- 5-quart slow cooker, combine cranberry-raspberry juice, apple cider, and the spice bag.

3. Cook while covered over low heat setting for around 4-6 hours or on a high heat setting for 2-2 1/2 hours.

4. Throw out the spice bag. Serve right away or keep it warm while covered on warm or low-heat setting up to 2 hours, occasionally stirring. Garnish each serving with apples (thinly sliced).

Nutrition: Calories 89 Carbs 22g Sugar 19g Protein: 15g; Fiber: 9g; Sodium: 256mg

119. Brunswick Stew

Preparation Time: 10 minutes

Cooking Time: 45 minutes

Serving: 3

Ingredients

- 4 ounces diced salt pork

- 2 pounds chicken parts

- 8 cups water

- 3 potatoes, cubed

- 3 onions, chopped

- 1 (28 ounce) can whole peeled tomatoes

- 2 cups canned whole kernel corn

- 1 (10 ounce) package frozen lima beans

- 1 tablespoon Worcestershire sauce

- 1/2 teaspoon salt

- 1/4 teaspoon ground black pepper

Direction

1. Mix and boil water, chicken and salt pork in a big pot on high heat. Lower heat to low. Cover then simmer until chicken is tender for 45 minutes.

2. Take out chicken. Let cool until easily handled. Take meat out. Throw out bones and skin. Chop meat to bite-sized pieces. Put back in the soup.

3. Add ground black pepper, salt, Worcestershire sauce, lima beans, corn, tomatoes, onions and potatoes. Mix well. Stir well and simmer for 1 hour, uncovered.

Nutrition: Calories 368 Carbs 27.9g Protein 25.9g Sugar: 15g; Fiber: 8g; Sodium: 375mg

120. Buffalo Chicken Salads

Preparation Time: 7 minutes

Cooking Time: 3 hours

Serving: 5

Ingredients

- 1½ pounds chicken breast halves

- ½ cup Wing Time® Buffalo chicken sauce

- 4 teaspoons cider vinegar

- 1 teaspoon Worcestershire sauce

- 1 teaspoon paprika

- 1/3 cup light mayonnaise

- 2 tablespoons fat-free milk

- 2 tablespoons crumbled blue cheese

- 2 romaine hearts, chopped

- 1 cup whole grain croutons

- ½ cup very thinly sliced red onion

Direction

1. Place chicken in a 2-quarts slow cooker. Mix together Worcestershire sauce, 2 teaspoons of vinegar and Buffalo sauce in a small bowl; pour over chicken. Dust with paprika. Close and cook for 3 hours on low-heat setting.

2. Mix the leftover 2 teaspoons of vinegar with milk and light mayonnaise together in a small bowl at serving time; mix in blue cheese. While chicken is still in the slow cooker, pull meat into bite-sized pieces using two forks.

3. Split the romaine among 6 dishes. Spoon sauce and chicken over lettuce. Pour with blue cheese dressing then add red onion slices and croutons on top.

Nutrition: Calories 274 Carbs 11g Fiber 2g Protein: 15g; Sugar: 11g; Sodium: 286mg

121. Cacciatore Style Chicken

Preparation Time: 10 minutes

Cooking Time: 4 hours

Serving: 6

Ingredients

- 2 cups sliced fresh mushrooms
- 1 cup sliced celery
- 1 cup chopped carrot
- 2 medium onions, cut into wedges
- 1 green, yellow, or red sweet peppers
- 4 cloves garlic, minced
- 12 chicken drumsticks
- ½ cup chicken broth
- ¼ cup dry white wine
- 2 tablespoons quick-cooking tapioca

- 2 bay leaves
- 1 teaspoon dried oregano, crushed
- 1 teaspoon sugar
- ½ teaspoon salt
- ¼ teaspoon pepper
- 1 (14.5 ounce) can diced tomatoes
- 1/3 cup tomato paste
- Hot cooked pasta or rice

Direction

1. Mix garlic, sweet pepper, onions, carrot, celery and mushrooms in a 5- or 6-qt. slow cooker. Cover veggies with the chicken. Add pepper, salt, sugar, oregano, bay leaves, tapioca, wine and broth.

2. Cover. Cook for 3–3 1/2 hours on high-heat setting.

3. Take chicken out; keep warm. Discard bay leaves. Turn to high-heat setting if using low-heat setting. Mix tomato paste and undrained tomatoes in. Cover. Cook on high-heat setting for 15 more minutes. Serving: Put veggie mixture on top of pasta and chicken.

Nutrition: Calories 324 Sugar: 7g Carbs 35g Protein: 15g; Fiber: 9g; Sodium: 358mg

122. Carnitas Tacos

Preparation Time: 10 minutes

Cooking Time: 5 hours

Serving: 4

Ingredients

- 3 to 3½-pound bone-in pork shoulder roast

- ½ cup chopped onion

- 1/3 cup orange juice

- 1 tablespoon ground cumin

- 1½ teaspoons kosher salt

- 1 teaspoon dried oregano, crushed

- ¼ teaspoon cayenne pepper

- 1 lime

- 2 (5.3 ounce) containers plain low-fat Greek yogurt

- 1 pinch kosher salt

- 16 (6 inch) soft yellow corn tortillas, such as Mission® brand

- 4 leaves green cabbage, quartered

- 1 cup very thinly sliced red onion

- 1 cup salsa (optional)

Direction

1. Take off meat from the bone; throw away bone. Trim meat fat. Slice meat into 2 to 3-inch pieces; put in a slow cooker of 3 1/2 or 4-quart in size. Mix in cayenne, oregano, salt, cumin, orange juice and onion.

2. Cover and cook for 4 to 5 hours on high. Take out meat from the cooker. Shred meat with two forks. Mix in enough cooking liquid to moisten.

3. Take out 1 teaspoon zest (put aside) for lime crema, then squeeze 2 tablespoons lime juice. Mix dash salt, yogurt, and lime juice in a small bowl.

4. Serve lime crema, salsa (if wished), red onion and cabbage with meat in tortillas. Scatter with lime zest.

Nutrition: Calories 301 Carbs 28g Sugar 7g Protein: 15g; Fiber: 9g; Sodium: 351mg

123. Chicken Chili

Preparation Time: 6 minutes

Cooking Time: 1 hour

Serving: 4

Ingredients

- 3 tablespoons vegetable oil

- 2 cloves garlic, minced

- 1 green bell pepper, chopped

- 1 onion, chopped

- 1 stalk celery, sliced

- 1/4-pound mushrooms, chopped

- 1-pound chicken breast

- 1 tablespoon chili powder

- 1 teaspoon dried oregano

- 1 teaspoon ground cumin

- 1/2 teaspoon paprika

- 1/2 teaspoon cocoa powder

- 1/4 teaspoon salt

- 1 pinch crushed red pepper flakes

- 1 pinch ground black pepper

- 1 (14.5 oz) can tomatoes with juice

- 1 (19 oz) can kidney beans

Direction

1. Fill 2 tablespoons of oil into a big skillet and heat it at moderate heat. Add mushrooms, celery, onion, bell pepper

and garlic, sautéing for 5 minutes. Put it to one side.

2. Insert the leftover 1 tablespoon of oil into the skillet. At high heat, cook the chicken until browned and its exterior turns firm. Transfer the vegetable mixture back into skillet.

3. Stir in ground black pepper, hot pepper flakes, salt, cocoa powder, paprika, oregano, cumin and chili powder. Continue stirring for several minutes to avoid burning. Pour in the beans and tomatoes and lead the entire mixture to boiling point then adjust the setting to low heat. Place a lid on the skillet and leave it simmering for 15 minutes. Uncover the skillet and leave it simmering for another 15 minutes.

Nutrition: Calories 308 Carbs 25.9g Protein 29g Sugar: 13g; Fiber: 9g; Sodium: 254mg

124. Chicken Vera Cruz

Preparation Time: 7 minutes

Cooking Time: 10 hours

Serving: 5

Ingredients

- 1 medium onion, cut into wedges

- 1-pound yellow-skin potatoes

- 6 skinless, boneless chicken thighs

- 2 (14.5 oz.) cans no-salt-added diced tomatoes

- 1 fresh jalapeño chili pepper

- 2 tablespoons Worcestershire sauce

- 1 tablespoon chopped garlic

- 1 teaspoon dried oregano, crushed

- ¼ teaspoon ground cinnamon

- 1/8 teaspoon ground cloves

- ½ cup snipped fresh parsley

- ¼ cup chopped pimiento-stuffed green olives

Direction

1. Put onion in a 3 1/2- or 4-quart slow cooker. Place chicken thighs and potatoes on top. Drain and discard juices from a can of tomatoes. Stir undrained and drained tomatoes, cloves, cinnamon, oregano, garlic, Worcestershire sauce and jalapeño pepper together in a bowl. Pour over all in the cooker.

2. Cook with a cover for 10 hours on low-heat setting.

3. To make the topping: Stir chopped pimiento-stuffed green olives and snipped fresh parsley together in a small bowl. Drizzle the topping over each serving of chicken.

Nutrition: Calories 228 Sugar 9g Carbs 25g Protein: 15g; Fiber 9g; Sodium: 396mg

125. Chicken and Cornmeal Dumplings

Preparation Time: 8 minutes

Cooking Time: 8 hours

Serving: 4

Ingredients

Chicken and Vegetable Filling

- 2 medium carrots, thinly sliced

- 1 stalk celery, thinly sliced

- 1/3 cup corn kernels

- ½ of a medium onion, thinly sliced

- 2 cloves garlic, minced

- 1 teaspoon snipped fresh rosemary

- ¼ teaspoon ground black pepper

- 2 chicken thighs, skinned

- 1 cup reduced sodium chicken broth

- ½ cup fat-free milk

- 1 tablespoon all-purpose flour

Cornmeal Dumplings

- ¼ cup flour

- ¼ cup cornmeal

- ½ teaspoon baking powder

- 1 egg white

- 1 tablespoon fat-free milk

- 1 tablespoon canola oil

Direction

1. Mix 1/4 teaspoon pepper, carrots, garlic, celery, rosemary, corn, and onion in a 1 1/2 or 2-quart slow cooker. Place chicken on top. Pour the broth atop mixture in the cooker.

2. Close and cook on low-heat for 7 to 8 hours.

3. If cooking with the low-heat setting, switch to high-heat setting (or if heat setting is not available, continue to cook). Place the chicken onto a cutting board and let to cool slightly. Once cool enough to handle, chop off chicken from bones and get rid of the bones. Chop the chicken and place back into the mixture in cooker. Mix flour and milk in a small bowl until smooth. Stir into the mixture in cooker.

4. Drop the Cornmeal Dumplings dough into 4 mounds atop hot chicken mixture using two spoons. Cover and cook for 20 to 25 minutes more or until a toothpick come out clean when inserted into a dumpling. (Avoid lifting lid when cooking.) Sprinkle each of the serving with coarse pepper if desired.

5. Mix together 1/2 teaspoon baking powder, 1/4 cup flour, a dash of salt and 1/4 cup cornmeal in a medium bowl. Mix 1 tablespoon canola oil, 1 egg white and 1 tablespoon fat-free milk in a small bowl. Pour the egg mixture into the flour mixture. Mix just until moistened.

Nutrition: Calories 369 Sugar 47g Carbs 9g Protein: 15g; Fiber: 11g; Sodium: 156mg

126. Chicken and Pepperoni

Preparation Time: 4 minutes

Cooking Time: 4 hours

Serving: 5

Ingredients

- 3½ to 4 pounds meaty chicken pieces

- 1/8 teaspoon salt

- 1/8 teaspoon black pepper

- 2 ounces sliced turkey pepperoni

- ¼ cup sliced pitted ripe olives

- ½ cup reduced-sodium chicken broth

- 1 tablespoon tomato paste

- 1 teaspoon dried Italian seasoning, crushed

- ½ cup shredded part-skim mozzarella cheese (2 ounces)

Direction

1. Put chicken into a 3 1/2 to 5-qt. slow cooker. Sprinkle pepper and salt on the chicken. Slice pepperoni slices in half. Put olives and pepperoni into the slow cooker. In a small bowl, blend Italian seasoning, tomato paste and chicken broth together. Transfer the mixture into the slow cooker.

2. Cook with a cover for 3-3 1/2 hours on high.

3. Transfer the olives, pepperoni and chicken onto a serving platter with a slotted spoon. Discard the cooking liquid. Sprinkle cheese over the chicken. Use foil to loosely cover and allow to sit for 5 minutes to melt the cheese.

Nutrition: Calories 243 Carbs 1g Protein 41g Sugar: 11g; Fiber: 6g; Sodium: 372mg

127.   Chicken and Sausage Gumbo

Preparation Time: 6 minutes

Cooking Time: 4 hours

Serving: 5

Ingredients

- 1/3 cup all-purpose flour

- 1 (14 ounce) can reduced-sodium chicken broth

- 2 cups chicken breast

- 8 ounces smoked turkey sausage links

- 2 cups sliced fresh okra

- 1 cup water

- 1 cup coarsely chopped onion

- 1 cup sweet pepper

- ½ cup sliced celery

- 4 cloves garlic, minced

- 1 teaspoon dried thyme

- ½ teaspoon ground black pepper

- ¼ teaspoon cayenne pepper

- 3 cups hot cooked brown rice

Direction

1. To make the roux: Cook the flour upon a medium heat in a heavy medium-sized saucepan, stirring periodically, for roughly 6 minutes or until the flour browns. Take off the heat and slightly cool, then slowly stir in the broth. Cook the roux until it bubbles and thickens up.

2. Pour the roux in a 3 1/2- or 4-quart slow cooker, then add in cayenne pepper, black pepper, thyme, garlic, celery, sweet pepper, onion, water, okra, sausage, and chicken.

3. Cook the soup covered on a high setting for 3 - 3 1/2 hours. Take the fat off the top and serve atop hot cooked brown rice.

Nutrition: Calories 230 Sugar 3g Protein 19g Carbs: 51g; Fiber: 9g; Sodium: 334mg

128.   Chicken, Barley, and Leek Stew

Preparation Time: 10 minutes

Cooking Time: 3 hours

Serving: 2

Ingredients

- 1-pound chicken thighs

- 1 tablespoon olive oil

- 1 (49 ounce) can reduced-sodium chicken broth

- 1 cup regular barley (not quick-cooking)

- 2 medium leeks, halved lengthwise and sliced

- 2 medium carrots, thinly sliced

- 1½ teaspoons dried basil or Italian seasoning, crushed

- ¼ teaspoon cracked black pepper

Direction

1. In the big skillet, cook the chicken in hot oil till becoming brown on all sides. In the 4-5-qt. slow cooker, whisk the pepper, dried basil, carrots, leeks, barley, chicken broth and chicken.

2. Keep covered and cooked over high heat setting for 2: 2.5 hours or till the barley softens. As you wish, drizzle with the parsley or fresh basil prior to serving.

Nutrition: Calories 248 Fiber 6g Carbs 27g Protein: 15g; Sugar: 11g; Fiber: 9g; Sodium: 369mg

129. Cider Pork Stew

Preparation Time: 9 minutes

Cooking Time: 12 hours

Serving: 3

Ingredients

- 2 pounds pork shoulder roast

- 3 medium cubed potatoes

- 3 medium carrots

- 2 medium onions, sliced

- 1 cup coarsely chopped apple

- ½ cup coarsely chopped celery

- 3 tablespoons quick-cooking tapioca

- 2 cups apple juice

- 1 teaspoon salt

- 1 teaspoon caraway seeds

- ¼ teaspoon black pepper

Direction

1. Chop the meat into 1-in. cubes. In the 3.5-5.5 qt. slow cooker, mix the tapioca, celery, apple, onions, carrots, potatoes and meat. Whisk in pepper, caraway seeds, salt and apple juice.

2. Keep covered and cook over low heat setting for 10-12 hours. If you want, use the celery leaves to decorate each of the servings.

Nutrition: Calories 244 Fiber 5g Carbs 33g Protein: 15g; Sugar: 11g; Fiber: 9g; Sodium: 396mg

130. Creamy Chicken Noodle Soup

Preparation Time: 7 minutes

Cooking Time: 8 hours

Serving: 4

Ingredients

- 1 (32 fluid ounce) container reduced-sodium chicken broth

- 3 cups water

- 2½ cups chopped cooked chicken

- 3 medium carrots, sliced

- 3 stalks celery

- 1½ cups sliced fresh mushrooms
- ¼ cup chopped onion
- 1½ teaspoons dried thyme, crushed
- ¾ teaspoon garlic-pepper seasoning
- 3 ounces reduced-fat cream cheese (Neufchâtel), cut up
- 2 cups dried egg noodles

Direction

1. Mix together the garlic-pepper seasoning, thyme, onion, mushrooms, celery, carrots, chicken, water and broth in a 5 to 6-quart slow cooker.

2. Put cover and let it cook for 6-8 hours on low-heat setting.

3. Increase to high-heat setting if you are using low-heat setting. Mix in the cream cheese until blended. Mix in uncooked noodles. Put cover and let it cook for an additional 20-30 minutes or just until the noodles become tender.

Nutrition: Calories 170 Sugar 3g Fiber 2g Protein: 15g; Carbs: 71g; Sodium: 275mg

131. Cuban Pulled Pork Sandwich

Preparation Time: 6 minutes

Cooking Time: 5 hours

Serving: 5

Ingredients

- 1 teaspoon dried oregano, crushed
- ¾ teaspoon ground cumin
- ½ teaspoon ground coriander
- ¼ teaspoon salt
- ¼ teaspoon black pepper

- ¼ teaspoon ground allspice
- 1 2 to 2½-pound boneless pork shoulder roast
- 1 tablespoon olive oil
- Nonstick cooking spray
- 2 cups sliced onions
- 2 green sweet peppers, cut into bite-size strips
- ½ to 1 fresh jalapeño pepper
- 4 cloves garlic, minced
- ¼ cup orange juice
- ¼ cup lime juice
- 6 heart-healthy wheat hamburger buns, toasted
- 2 tablespoons jalapeño mustard

Direction

1. Mix allspice, oregano, black pepper, cumin, salt, and coriander together in a small bowl. Press each side of the roast into the spice mixture. On medium-high heat, heat oil in a big non-stick pan; put in roast. Cook for 5mins until both sides of the roast is light brown, turn the roast one time.

2. Using a cooking spray, grease a 3 1/2 or 4qt slow cooker; arrange the garlic, onions, jalapeno, and green peppers in a layer. Pour in lime juice and orange juice. Slice the roast if needed to fit inside the cooker; put on top of the vegetables covered or 4 1/2-5hrs on high heat setting.

3. Move roast to a cutting board using a slotted spoon. Drain the cooking liquid and keep the jalapeno, green peppers, and onions. Shred the roast with 2 forks

then place it back in the cooker. Remove fat from the liquid. Mix half cup of cooking liquid and reserved vegetables into the cooker. Pour in more cooking liquid if desired. Discard the remaining cooking liquid.

4. Slather mustard on rolls. Split the meat between the bottom roll halves. Add avocado on top if desired. Place the roll tops to sandwiches.

Nutrition: Calories 379 Carbs 32g Fiber 4g Protein: 15g; Sugar: 7g; Sodium: 318mg

Seafood Recipes

132. Shrimp with Green Beans

Preparation Time: 10 minutes

Cooking Time: 2 Minutes

Servings: 4

Ingredients:

- ¾ pound fresh green beans, trimmed

- 1 pound medium frozen shrimp, peeled and deveined

- 2 tablespoons fresh lemon juice

- 2 tablespoons olive oil

- Salt and ground black pepper, as required

Directions:

1. Arrange a steamer trivet in the Instant Pot and pour cup of water.

2. Arrange the green beans on top of trivet in a single layer and top with shrimp.

3. Drizzle with oil and lemon juice.

4. Sprinkle with salt and black pepper.

5. Close the lid and place the pressure valve to "Seal" position.

6. Press "Steam" and just use the default time of 2 minutes.

7. Press "Cancel" and allow a "Natural" release.

8. Open the lid and serve.

Nutrition: Calories: 223, Fats: 1g, Carbs: 7.9g, Sugar: 1.4g, Proteins: 27.4g, Sodium: 322mg

133. Crab Curry

Preparation Time: 10 minutes

Cooking Time: 20 Minutes

Servings: 2

Ingredients:

- 0.5lb chopped crab

- 1 thinly sliced red onion

- 0.5 cup chopped tomato

- 3tbsp curry paste

- 1tbsp oil or ghee

Directions:

1. Set the Instant Pot to sauté and add the onion, oil, and curry paste.

2. When the onion is soft, add the remaining ingredients and seal.

3. Cook on Stew for 20 minutes.

4. Release the pressure naturally.

Nutrition: Calories: 223, Fats: 1g, Carbs: 7.9g, Sugar: 1.4g, Proteins: 27.4g, Sodium: 322mg Fiber: 9g;

134.   Mixed Chowder

Preparation Time: 10 minutes

Cooking Time: 35 Minutes

Servings: 2

Ingredients:

- 1lb fish stew mix
- 2 cups white sauce
- 3tbsp old bay seasoning

Directions:

1. Mix all the ingredients in your Instant Pot.
2. Cook on Stew for 35 minutes.
3. Release the pressure naturally.

Nutrition: Calories: 320; Carbs: 9; Sugar: 2; Fat: 16; Protein: 4, Fiber: 9g; Sodium: 279mg

135.   Mussels in Tomato Sauce

Preparation Time: 10 minutes

Cooking Time: 3 Minutes

Servings: 4

Ingredients:

- 2 tomatoes, seeded and chopped finely
- 2 pounds mussels, scrubbed and de-bearded
- 1 cup low-sodium chicken broth
- 1 tablespoon fresh lemon juice
- 2 garlic cloves, minced

Directions:

1. In the pot of Instant Pot, place tomatoes, garlic, wine and bay leaf and stir to combine.
2. Arrange the mussels on top.
3. Close the lid and place the pressure valve to "Seal" position.
4. Press "Manual" and cook under "High Pressure" for about 3 minutes.
5. Press "Cancel" and carefully allow a "Quick" release.
6. Open the lid and serve hot.

Nutrition: Calories: 213, Fats: 25.2g, Carbs: 11g, Sugar: 1. Proteins: 28.2g, Fiber: 11g.

136.   Citrus Salmon

Preparation Time: 10 minutes

Cooking Time: 7 Minutes

Servings: 4

Ingredients:

- 4 (4-ounce) salmon fillets
- 1 cup low-sodium chicken broth
- 1 teaspoon fresh ginger, minced
- 2 teaspoons fresh orange zest, grated finely
- 3 tablespoons fresh orange juice
- 1 tablespoon olive oil
- Ground black pepper, as required

Directions:

1. In Instant Pot, add all ingredients and mix.

2. Close the lid and place the pressure valve to "Seal" position.

3. Press "Manual" and cook under "High Pressure" for about 7 minutes.

4. Press "Cancel" and allow a "Natural" release.

5. Open the lid and serve the salmon fillets with the topping of cooking sauce.

Nutrition: Calories: 190, Fats: 10.5g, Carbs: 1.8g, Sugar: 1g, Proteins: 22. Sodium: 68mg Fiber: 9g.

137. Herbed Salmon

Preparation Time: 10 minutes

Cooking Time: 3 Minutes

Servings: 4

Ingredients:

- 4 (4-ounce) salmon fillets
- ¼ cup olive oil
- 2 tablespoons fresh lemon juice
- 1 garlic clove, minced
- ¼ teaspoon dried oregano
- Salt and ground black pepper, as required
- 4 fresh rosemary sprigs
- 4 lemon slices

Directions:

1. For dressing: in a large bowl, add oil, lemon juice, garlic, oregano, salt and black pepper and beat until well co combined.

2. Arrange a steamer trivet in the Instant Pot and pour 11/2 cups of water in Instant Pot.

3. Place the salmon fillets on top of trivet in a single layer and top with dressing.

4. Arrange 1 rosemary sprig and 1 lemon slice over each fillet.

5. Close the lid and place the pressure valve to "Seal" position.

6. Press "Steam" and just use the default time of 3 minutes.

7. Press "Cancel" and carefully allow a "Quick" release.

8. Open the lid and serve hot.

Nutrition: Calories: 262, Fats: 17g, Carbs: 0.7g, Sugar: 0.2g, Proteins: 22.1g, Sodium: 91mg Fiber: 9g;

138. Salmon in Green Sauce

Preparation Time: 10 minutes

Cooking Time: 12 Minutes

Servings: 4

Ingredients:

- 4 (6-ounce) salmon fillets
- 1 avocado, peeled, pitted and chopped
- 1/2 cup fresh basil, chopped
- 3 garlic cloves, chopped
- 1 tablespoon fresh lemon zest, grated finely

Directions:

1. Grease a large piece of foil.

2. In a large bowl, add all ingredients except salmon and water and with a fork, mash completely.

3. Place fillets in the center of foil and top with avocado mixture evenly.

4. Fold the foil around fillets to seal them.

5. Arrange a steamer trivet in the Instant Pot and pour 1/2 cup of water.

6. Place the foil packet on top of trivet.

7. Close the lid and place the pressure valve to "Seal" position.

8. Press "Manual" and cook under "High Pressure" for about minutes.

9. Meanwhile, preheat the oven to broiler.

10. Press "Cancel" and allow a "Natural" release.

11. Open the lid and transfer the salmon fillets onto a broiler pan.

12. Broil for about 3-4 minutes.

13. Serve warm.

Nutrition: Calories: 333, Fats: 20.3g, Carbs: 5.5g, Sugar: 0.4g, Proteins: 34.2g, Sodium: 79mg; Fiber: 11g;

139. Braised Shrimp

Preparation Time: 10 minutes

Cooking Time: 4 Minutes

Servings: 4

Ingredients:

- 1 pound frozen large shrimp, peeled and deveined

- 2 shallots, chopped

- ¾ cup low-sodium chicken broth

- 2 tablespoons fresh lemon juice

- 2 tablespoons olive oil

- 1 tablespoon garlic, crushed

- Ground black pepper, as required

Directions:

1. In the Instant Pot, place oil and press "Sauté". Now add the shallots and cook for about 2 minutes.

2. Add the garlic and cook for about 1 minute.

3. Press "Cancel" and stir in the shrimp, broth, lemon juice and black pepper.

4. Close the lid and place the pressure valve to "Seal" position.

5. Press "Manual" and cook under "High Pressure" for about 1 minute.

6. Press "Cancel" and carefully allow a "Quick" release.

7. Open the lid and serve hot.

Nutrition: Calories: 209, Fats: 9g, Carbs: 4.3g, Sugar: 0.2g, Proteins: 26.6g, Sodium: 293mg Fiber: 10g;

140. Shrimp Coconut Curry

Preparation Time: 10 minutes

Cooking Time: 20 Minutes

Servings: 2

Ingredients:

- 0.5lb cooked shrimp

- 1 thinly sliced onion

- 1 cup coconut yogurt

- 3tbsp curry paste

- 1tbsp oil or ghee

Directions:

1. Set the Instant Pot to sauté and add the onion, oil, and curry paste.

2. When the onion is soft, add the remaining ingredients and seal.

3. Cook on Stew for 20 minutes.

4. Release the pressure naturally.

Nutrition: Calories: 380; Carbs: 13; Sugar: 4; Fat: 22; Protein: 40; Fiber: 9g; Sodium: 318mg

141.   Trout Bake

Preparation Time: 10 minutes

Cooking Time: 35 Minutes

Servings: 2

Ingredients:

- 1lb trout fillets, boneless

- 1lb chopped winter vegetables

- 1 cup low sodium fish broth

- 1tbsp mixed herbs

- sea salt as desired

Directions:

1. Mix all the ingredients except the broth in a foil pouch.

2. Place the pouch in the steamer basket your Instant Pot.

3. Pour the broth into the Instant Pot.

4. Cook on Steam for 35 minutes.

5. Release the pressure naturally.

Nutrition: Calories: 310; Carbs: 14; Sugar: 2; Fat: 12; Protein: 40; Fiber: 9g; Sodium: 288mg

142.   Sardine Curry

Preparation Time: 10 minutes

Cooking Time: 35 Minutes

Servings: 2

Ingredients:

- 5 tins of sardines in tomato

- 1lb chopped vegetables

- 1 cup low sodium fish broth

- 3tbsp curry paste

Directions:

1. Mix all the ingredients in your Instant Pot.

2. Cook on Stew for 35 minutes.

3. Release the pressure naturally.

Nutrition: Calories: 320; Carbs: 8; Sugar: 2; Fat: 16; Protein: 3g Fiber: 9g; sodium:284mg

143.   Swordfish Steak

Preparation Time: 10 minutes

Cooking Time: 35 Minutes

Servings: 2

Ingredients:

- 1lb swordfish steak, whole

- 1lb chopped Mediterranean vegetables

- 1 cup low sodium fish broth

- 2tbsp soy sauce

Directions:

1. Mix all the ingredients except the broth in a foil pouch.

2. Place the pouch in the steamer basket for your Instant Pot.

3. Pour the broth into the Instant Pot. Lower the steamer basket into the Instant Pot.

4. Cook on Steam for 35 minutes.

5. Release the pressure naturally.

Nutrition: Calories: 270; Carbs: 5; Sugar: 1; Fat: 10; Protein: 48; GL: 1

144.   Lemon Sole

Preparation Time: 10 minutes

Cooking Time: 5 Minutes

Servings: 2

Ingredients:

- 1lb sole fillets, boned and skinned

- 1 cup low sodium fish broth

- 2 shredded sweet onions

- juice of half a lemon

- 2tbsp dried cilantro

Directions:

1. Mix all the ingredients in your Instant Pot.

2. Cook on Stew for 5 minutes.

3. Release the pressure naturally.

Nutrition: Calories: 270; Carbs: 5; Sugar: 1; Fat: 10; Protein: 48; Fiber: 11g; Sodium: 329mg

145.   Lemony Salmon

Preparation Time: 10 minutes

Cooking Time: 3 Minutes

Servings: 3

Ingredients:

- 1 pound salmon fillet, cut into 3 pieces

- 3 teaspoons fresh dill, chopped

- 5 tablespoons fresh lemon juice, divided

- Salt and ground black pepper, as required

Directions:

1. Arrange a steamer trivet in Instant Pot and pour ¼ cup of lemon juice.

2. Season the salmon with salt and black pepper evenly.

3. Place the salmon pieces on top of trivet, skin side down and drizzle with remaining lemon juice.

4. Now, sprinkle the salmon pieces with dill evenly.

5. Close the lid and place the pressure valve to "Seal" position.

6. Press "Steam" and use the default time of 3 minutes.

7. Press "Cancel" and allow a "Natural" release.

8. Open the lid and serve hot.

Nutrition: Calories: 230; Carbs: Sugar: 1; Fat: 6; Protein: 46; Fiber: 16g; Sodium: 285mg

146.   Tuna Sweet corn Casserole

Preparation Time: 10 minutes

Cooking Time: 35 Minutes

Servings: 2

Ingredients:

- 3 small tins of tuna
- 0.5lb sweet corn kernels
- 1lb chopped vegetables
- 1 cup low sodium vegetable broth
- 2tbsp spicy seasoning

Directions:

1. Mix all the ingredients in your Instant Pot.
2. Cook on Stew for 35 minutes.
3. Release the pressure naturally.

Nutrition: Calories: 300; Carbs: 6; Sugar: 1; Fat: 9; Protein: 45 Fiber: 12g; Sodium: 287mg.

147. Lemon Pepper Salmon

Preparation Time: 10 minutes

Cooking Time: 10 Minutes

Servings: 4

Ingredients:

- 3 tbsps. ghee or avocado oil
- 1 lb. skin-on salmon filet
- 1 julienned red bell pepper
- 1 julienned green zucchini
- 1 julienned carrot
- ¾ cup water
- A few sprigs of parsley, tarragon, dill, basil or a combination
- 1/2 sliced lemon
- 1/2 tsp. black pepper
- ¼ tsp. sea salt

Directions:

1. Add the water and the herbs into the bottom of the Instant Pot and put in a wire steamer rack making sure the handles extend upwards.
2. Place the salmon filet onto the wire rack, with the skin side facing down.
3. Drizzle the salmon with ghee, season with black pepper and salt, and top with the lemon slices.
4. Close and seal the Instant Pot, making sure the vent is turned to "Sealing".
5. Select the "Steam" setting and cook for 3 minutes.
6. While the salmon cooks, julienne the vegetables, and set aside.
7. Once done, quick release the pressure, and then press the "Keep Warm/Cancel" button.
8. Uncover and wearing oven mitts, carefully remove the steamer rack with the salmon.
9. Remove the herbs and discard them.
10. Add the vegetables to the pot and put the lid back on.
11. Select the "Sauté" function and cook for 1-2 minutes.
12. Serve the vegetables with salmon and add the remaining fat to the pot.
13. Pour a little of the sauce over the fish and vegetables if desired.

Nutrition: Calories 296, Carbs 8g, Fat 15 g, Protein 31 g, Fiber 12g, Sodium 284 mg

148. Baked Salmon with Garlic Parmesan Topping

Preparation time: 5 minutes,

Cooking time: 20 minutes,

Servings: 4

Ingredients:

- 1 lb. wild caught salmon filets

- 2 tbsp. margarine

- What you'll need from store cupboard:

- ¼ cup reduced fat parmesan cheese, grated

- ¼ cup light mayonnaise

- 2-3 cloves garlic, diced

- 2 tbsp. parsley

- Salt and pepper

Directions:

1. Heat oven to 350 and line a baking pan with parchment paper.

2. Place salmon on pan and season with salt and pepper.

3. In a medium skillet, over medium heat, melt butter. Add garlic and cook, stirring 1 minute.

4. Reduce heat to low and add remaining Ingredients. Stir until everything is melted and combined.

5. Spread evenly over salmon and bake 15 minutes for thawed fish or 20 for frozen. Salmon is done when it flakes easily with a fork. Serve.

Nutrition: Calories 408 Carbs 4g Protein 41g Fat 24g Sugar 1g Fiber 0g Sodium: 228mg

149. Blackened Shrimp

Preparation time: 5 minutes

Cooking time: 5 minutes

Servings: 4

Ingredients:

- 1 1/2 lbs. shrimp, peel & devein

- 4 lime wedges

- 4 tbsp. cilantro, chopped

- What you'll need from store cupboard:

- 4 cloves garlic, diced

- 1 tbsp. chili powder

- 1 tbsp. paprika

- 1 tbsp. olive oil

- 2 tsp. Splenda brown sugar

- 1 tsp. cumin

- 1 tsp. oregano

- 1 tsp. garlic powder

- 1 tsp. salt

- 1/2 tsp. pepper

Directions:

1. In a small bowl combine seasonings and Splenda brown sugar.

2. Heat oil in a skillet over med-high heat. Add shrimp, in a single layer, and cook 1-2 minutes per side.

3. Add seasonings, and cook, stirring, 30 seconds. Serve garnished with cilantro and a lime wedge.

Nutrition: Calories 252 Carbs 7g Protein 39g Fat 7g Sugar 2g Fiber 1g; Sodium: 396mg

150. Cajun Catfish

Preparation time: 5 minutes

Cooking time: 15 minutes

Servings: 4

Ingredients:

- 4 (8 oz.) catfish fillets
- What you'll need from store cupboard:
- 2 tbsp. olive oil
- 2 tsp. garlic salt
- 2 tsp. thyme
- 2 tsp. paprika
- 1/2 tsp. cayenne pepper
- 1/2 tsp. red hot sauce
- ¼ tsp. black pepper
- Nonstick cooking spray

Directions:

1. Heat oven to 450 degrees. Spray a 9x13-inch baking dish with cooking spray.

2. In a small bowl whisk together everything but catfish. Brush both sides of fillets, using all the spice mix.

3. Bake 10-13 minutes or until fish flakes easily with a fork. Serve.

Nutrition: Calories 366 Carbs 0g Protein 35g Fat 24g Sugar 0g Fiber 0g Sodium: 288mg

151. Cajun Flounder & Tomatoes

Preparation time: 10 minutes

Cooking time: 15 minutes

Servings: 4

Ingredients:

- 4 flounder fillets
- 2 1/2 cups tomatoes, diced
- ¾ cup onion, diced
- ¾ cup green bell pepper, diced
- What you'll need from store cupboard:
- 2 cloves garlic, diced fine
- 1 tbsp. Cajun seasoning
- 1 tsp. olive oil

Directions:

1. Heat oil in a large skillet over med-high heat. Add onion and garlic and cook 2 minutes, or until soft. Add tomatoes, peppers and spices, and cook 2-3 minutes until tomatoes soften.

2. Lay fish over top. Cover, reduce heat to medium and cook, 5-8 minutes, or until fish flakes easily with a fork. Transfer fish to serving plates and top with sauce.

Nutrition: Calories 194 Carbs 8g Protein 32g Fat 3g Sugar 5g Fiber 2g Sodium: 227mg

152. Cajun Shrimp & Roasted Vegetables

Preparation time: 5 minutes

Cooking time: 15 minutes

Servings: 4

Ingredients:

- 1 lb. large shrimp, peeled and deveined

- 2 zucchinis, sliced
- 2 yellow squash, sliced
- 1/2 bunch asparagus, cut into thirds
- 2 red bell pepper, cut into chunks
- What you'll need from store cupboard:
- 2 tbsp. olive oil
- 2 tbsp. Cajun Seasoning
- Salt & pepper, to taste

Directions:

1. Heat oven to 400 degrees.
2. Combine shrimp and vegetables in a large bowl. Add oil and seasoning and toss to coat.
3. Spread evenly in a large baking sheet and bake 15-20 minutes, or until vegetables are tender. Serve.

Nutrition: Calories 251 Carbs 13g Protein 30g Fat 9g Sugar 6g Fiber 4g Sodium: 257mg

153.   Cilantro Lime Grilled Shrimp

Preparation time: 5 minutes,

Cooking time: 5 minutes,

Servings: 6

Ingredients:

- 1 1/2 lbs. large shrimp raw, peeled, deveined with tails on
- Juice and zest of 1 lime
- 2 tbsp. fresh cilantro chopped
- What you'll need from store cupboard:
- ¼ cup olive oil

- 2 cloves garlic, diced fine
- 1 tsp. smoked paprika
- ¼ tsp. cumin
- 1/2 teaspoon salt
- ¼ tsp. cayenne pepper

Directions:

1. Place the shrimp in a large Ziploc bag.
2. Mix remaining Ingredients in a small bowl and pour over shrimp. Let marinate 20-30 minutes.
3. Heat up the grill. Skewer the shrimp and cook 2-3 minutes, per side, just until they turn pick. Be careful not to overcook them. Serve garnished with cilantro.

Nutrition: Calories 317 Carbs 4g Protein 39g Fat 15g Sugar 0g Fiber 0g Sodium: 396mg

154.   Crab Frittata

Preparation time: 10 minutes

Cooking time: 50 minutes

Servings: 4

Ingredients:

- 4 eggs
- 2 cups lump crabmeat
- 1 cup half-n-half
- 1 cup green onions, diced
- What you'll need from store cupboard:
- 1 cup reduced fat parmesan cheese, grated
- 1 tsp. salt

- 1 tsp. pepper

- 1 tsp. smoked paprika

- 1 tsp. Italian seasoning

- Nonstick cooking spray

Directions:

1. Heat oven to 350 degrees. Spray an 8-inch springform pan, or pie plate with cooking spray.

2. In a large bowl, whisk together the eggs and half-n-half. Add seasonings and parmesan cheese, stir to mix.

3. Stir in the onions and crab meat. Pour into prepared pan and bake 35-40 minutes, or eggs are set and top is lightly browned.

4. Let cool 10 minutes, then slice and serve warm or at room temperature.

Nutrition: Calories 276 Carbs 5g Protein 25g Fat 17g Sugar 1g Fiber 1g Sodium: 287mg

Appetizers and Snacks

155.   Brussels Sprouts

Preparation Time: 5 minutes

Cooking Time: 3 minutes

Servings: 5

Ingredients:

- 1 tsp. extra-virgin olive oil

- 1 lb. halved Brussels sprouts

- 3 tbsps. apple cider vinegar

- 3 tbsps. gluten-free tamari soy sauce

- 3 tbsps. chopped sun-dried tomatoes

Direction:

1. Select the "Sauté" function on your Instant Pot, add oil and allow the pot to get hot.

2. Cancel the "Sauté" function and add the Brussels sprouts.

3. Stir well and allow the sprouts to cook in the residual heat for 2-3 minutes.

4. Add the tamari soy sauce and vinegar, and then stir.

5. Cover the Instant Pot, sealing the pressure valve by pointing it to "Sealing."

6. Select the "Manual, High Pressure" setting and cook for 3 minutes.

7. Once the cook cycle is done, do a quick pressure release, and then stir in the chopped sun-dried tomatoes.

8. Serve immediately.

Nutrition: Calories 62 Carbs 10g Fat 1g Protein: 15g; Sugar: 11g; Fiber: 9g; Sodium: 396mg

156. Garlic and Herb Carrots

Preparation Time: 2 minutes

Cooking Time: 18 minutes

Servings: 3

Ingredients:

- 2 tbsps. butter
- 1 lb. baby carrots
- 1 cup water
- 1 tsp. fresh thyme or oregano
- 1 tsp. minced garlic
- Black pepper
- Coarse sea salt

Direction:

1. Fill water to the inner pot of the Instant Pot, and then put in a steamer basket.

2. .Layer the carrots into the steamer basket.

3. Close and seal the lid, with the pressure vent in the "Sealing" position.

4. Select the "Steam" setting and cook for 2 minutes on high pressure.

5. Quick release the pressure and then carefully remove the steamer basket with the steamed carrots, discarding the water.

6. Add butter to the inner pot of the Instant Pot and allow it to melt on the "Sauté" function.

7. Add garlic and sauté for 30 seconds, and then add the carrots. Mix well.

8. Stir in the fresh herbs, and cook for 2-3 minutes.

9. Season with salt and black pepper, and the transfer to a serving bowl.

10. .Serve warm and enjoy!

Nutrition: Calories 122 Carbs 12g Fat 7g Protein: 15g; Sugar: 10g; Fiber: 19g; Sodium: 322mg

157. Cilantro Lime Drumsticks

Preparation Time: 5 minutes

Cooking Time: 15 minutes

Servings: 6

Ingredients:

- 1 tbsp. olive oil
- 6 chicken drumsticks
- 4 minced garlic cloves
- ½ cup low-sodium chicken broth
- 1 tsp. cayenne pepper
- 1 tsp. crushed red peppers
- 1 tsp. fine sea salt
- Juice of 1 lime

To Serve:

- 2 tbsp. chopped cilantro
- Extra lime zest

Direction:

1. Pour olive oil to the Instant Pot and set it on the "Sauté" function.

2. Once the oil is hot adding the chicken drumsticks, and season them well.

3. Using tongs, stir the drumsticks and brown the drumsticks for 2 minutes per side.

4. Add the lime juice, fresh cilantro, and chicken broth to the pot.

5. Lock and seal the lid, turning the pressure valve to "Sealing."

6. Cook the drumsticks on the "Manual, High Pressure" setting for 9 minutes.

7. Once done let the pressure release naturally.

8. Carefully transfer the drumsticks to an aluminum-foiled baking sheet and broil them in the oven for 3-5 minutes until golden brown.

9. Serve warm, garnished with more cilantro and lime zest.

Nutrition: Calories 480 Carbs 3.3g Fat 29g Protein: 15g; Sugar: 13g; Fiber: 18g; Sodium: 320mg

158.   Eggplant Spread

Preparation Time: 5 minutes

Cooking Time: 18 minutes

Servings: 5

Ingredients:

- 4 tbsps. extra-virgin olive oil

- 2 lbs. eggplant

- 4 skin-on garlic cloves

- ½ cup water

- ¼ cup pitted black olives

- 3 sprigs fresh thyme

- Juice of 1 lemon

- 1 tbsp. tahini

- 1 tsp. sea salt

- Fresh extra-virgin olive oil

Direction:

1. Peel the eggplant in alternating stripes, leaving some areas with skin and some with no skin.

2. Slice into big chunks and layer at the bottom of your Instant Pot.

3. Add olive oil to the pot, and on the "Sauté" function, fry and caramelize the eggplant on one side, about 5 minutes.

4. Add in the garlic cloves with the skin on.

5. Flip over the eggplant and then add in the remaining uncooked eggplant chunks, salt, and water.

6. Close the lid, ensure the pressure release valve is set to "Sealing."

7. Cook for 5 minutes on the "Manual, High Pressure" setting.

8. Once done, carefully open the pot by quick releasing the pressure through the steam valve.

9. Discard most of the brown cooking liquid.

10. Remove the garlic cloves and peel them.

11. Add the lemon juice, tahini, cooked and fresh garlic cloves and pitted black olives to the pot.

12. Using a hand-held immersion blender, process all the ingredients until smooth.

13. Pour out the spread into a serving dish and season with fresh thyme, whole black olives and some extra-virgin olive oil, prior to serving.

Nutrition: Calories 155 Carbs 16.8g Fat 11.7g Protein: 27g; Sugar: 19g; Fiber: 28g; Sodium: 313mg

159. Carrot Hummus

Preparation Time: 15 minutes

Cooking Time: 10 minutes

Servings: 2

Ingredients:

- 1 chopped carrot
- 2 oz. cooked chickpeas
- 1 tsp. lemon juice
- 1 tsp. tahini
- 1 tsp. fresh parsley

Direction:

1. Place the carrot and chickpeas in your Instant Pot.
2. Add a cup of water, seal, cook for 10 minutes on Stew.
3. Depressurize naturally. Blend with the remaining ingredients.

Nutrition: Calories 58 Carbs 8g Fat 2g Protein: 11g; Sugar: 15g; Fiber: 12g; Sodium: 372mg

160. Vegetable Rice Pilaf

Preparation Time: 5 minutes

Cooking Time: 25 minutes

Servings: 6

Ingredients:

- 1 tablespoon olive oil
- ½ medium yellow onion, diced
- 1 cup uncooked long-grain brown rice
- 2 cloves minced garlic
- ½ teaspoon dried basil
- Salt and pepper
- 2 cups fat-free chicken broth
- 1 cup frozen mixed veggies

Direction:

1. Cook oil in a large skillet over medium heat.
2. Add the onion and sauté for 3 minutes until translucent.
3. Stir in the rice and cook until lightly toasted.
4. Add the garlic, basil, salt, and pepper then stir to combined.
5. Stir in the chicken broth then bring to a boil.
6. Decrease heat and simmer, covered, for 10 minutes.
7. Stir in the frozen veggies then cover and cook for another 10 minutes until heated through. Serve hot.

Nutrition: Calories 90 Carbs 12.6g Protein: 12.5g; Sugar: 14.1g; Fiber: 9.6g; Sodium: 321.3mg

161. Curry Roasted Cauliflower Florets

Preparation Time: 5 minutes

Cooking Time: 25 minutes

Servings: 6

Ingredients:

- 8 cups cauliflower florets
- 2 tablespoons olive oil
- 1 teaspoon curry powder
- ½ teaspoon garlic powder
- Salt and pepper

Direction:

1. Prep the oven to 425°F and line a baking sheet with foil.
2. Toss the cauliflower with the olive oil and spread on the baking sheet.
3. Sprinkle with curry powder, garlic powder, salt, and pepper.
4. Roast for 25 minutes or until just tender. Serve hot.

Nutrition: Calories 75 Carbs 7.4g Fiber 3.5g Protein: 15g; Sugar: 11g; Fiber: 9g; Sodium: 396mg

162.   Mushroom Barley Risotto

Preparation Time: 5 minutes

Cooking Time: 25 minutes

Servings: 8

Ingredients:

- 4 cups fat-free beef broth
- 2 tablespoons olive oil
- 1 small onion, diced well
- 2 cloves minced garlic
- 8 ounces thinly sliced mushrooms
- ¼ tsp dried thyme
- Salt and pepper
- 1 cup pearled barley
- ½ cup dry white wine

Direction:

1. Heat the beef broth in a medium saucepan and keep it warm.
2. Heat the oil in a large, deep skillet over medium heat.
3. Add the onions and garlic and sauté for 2 minutes then stir in the mushrooms and thyme.
4. Season with salt and pepper and sauté for 2 minutes more.
5. Add the barley and sauté for 1 minute then pour in the wine.
6. Ladle about ½ cup of beef broth into the skillet and stir well to combine.
7. Cook until most of the broth has been absorbed then add another ladle.
8. Repeat until you have used all of the broth and the barley is cooked to al dente.
9. Season and serve hot.

Nutrition: Calories 155 Carbs 21.9g Fiber 4.4g Protein: 15g; Sugar: 11g; Fiber:11.2g; Sodium: 396mg

163.   Lemon Garlic Green Beans

Preparation time: 5 minutes

Cooking Time: 10 minutes

Servings: 6

Ingredients:

- 1 1/2 pounds green beans, trimmed

- 2 tablespoons olive oil

- 1 tablespoon fresh lemon juice

- 2 cloves minced garlic

- Salt and pepper

Directions:

1. Fill a large bowl with ice water and set aside.

2. Bring a pot of salted water to boil then add the green beans.

3. Cook for 3 minutes then drain and immediately place in the ice water.

4. Cool the beans completely then drain them well.

5. Heat the oil in a large skillet over medium-high heat.

6. Add the green beans, tossing to coat, then add the lemon juice, garlic, salt, and pepper.

7. Sauté for 3 minutes until the beans are tender-crisp then serve hot.

Nutrition: Calories 75, Fat 4.8g, Carbs 8.5g, Protein 2.1g, Sugar 1.7g, Fiber 3.9g, Sodium 7mg

164. Brown Rice & Lentil Salad

Preparation time: 10 minutes

Cooking Time: 10 minutes

Servings: 4

Ingredients:

- 1 cup water

- 1/2 cup instant brown rice

- 2 tablespoons olive oil

- 2 tablespoons red wine vinegar

- 1 tablespoon Dijon mustard

- 1 tablespoon minced onion

- 1/2 teaspoon paprika

- Salt and pepper

- 1 (15-ounce) can brown lentils, rinsed and drained

- 1 medium carrot, shredded

- 2 tablespoons fresh chopped parsley

Directions:

1. Stir together the water and instant brown rice in a medium saucepan.

2. Bring to a boil then simmer for 10 minutes, covered.

3. Remove from heat and set aside while you prepare the salad.

4. Whisk together the olive oil, vinegar, Dijon mustard, onion, paprika, salt, and pepper in a medium bowl.

5. Toss in the cooked rice, lentils, carrots, and parsley.

6. Adjust seasoning to taste then stir well and serve warm.

Nutrition: Calories 145, Fat 7.7g, Carbs 13.1g, Protein 6g, Sugar 1g, Fiber 2.2g, Sodium 57mg

165. Mashed Butternut Squash

Preparation time: 5 minutes

Cooking Time: 25 minutes

Servings: 6

Ingredients:

- 3 pounds whole butternut squash (about 2 medium)

- 2 tablespoons olive oil

- Salt and pepper

Directions:

1. Preheat the oven to 400F and line a baking sheet with parchment.

2. Cut the squash in half and remove the seeds.

3. Cut the squash into cubes and toss with oil then spread on the baking sheet.

4. Roast for 25 minutes until tender then place in a food processor.

5. Blend smooth then season with salt and pepper to taste.

Nutrition: Calories 90, Fat 4.8g, Carbs 12.3g, Protein 1.1g, Sugar 2.3g, Fiber 2.1g, Sodium 4mg

166. Cilantro Lime Quinoa

Preparation time: 5 minutes

Cooking Time: 25 minutes

Servings: 6

Ingredients:

- 1 cup uncooked quinoa

- 1 tablespoon olive oil

- 1 medium yellow onion, diced

- 2 cloves minced garlic

- 1 (4-ounce) can diced green chiles, drained

- 1 1/2 cups fat-free chicken broth

- ¾ cup fresh chopped cilantro

- 1/2 cup sliced green onion

- 2 tablespoons lime juice

- Salt and pepper

Directions:

1. Rinse the quinoa thoroughly in cool water using a fine mesh sieve.

2. Heat the oil in a large saucepan over medium heat.

3. Add the onion and sauté for 2 minutes then stir in the chile and garlic.

4. Cook for 1 minute then stir in the quinoa and chicken broth.

5. Bring to a boil then reduce heat and simmer, covered, until the quinoa absorbs the liquid: about 20 to 25 minutes.

6. Remove from heat then stir in the cilantro, green onions, and lime juice.

7. Season with salt and pepper to taste and serve hot.

Nutrition: Calories 150, Fat 4.1g, Carbs 22.5g, Protein 6g, Sugar 1.7g, Fiber 2.7g, Sodium 179mg

167. Oven-Roasted Veggies

Preparation time: 5 minutes

Cooking Time: 25 minutes

Servings: 6

Ingredients:

- 1 pound cauliflower florets

- 1/2 pound broccoli florets

- 1 large yellow onion, cut into chunks

- 1 large red pepper, cored and chopped

- 2 medium carrots, peeled and sliced
- 2 tablespoons olive oil
- 2 tablespoons apple cider vinegar
- Salt and pepper

Directions:

1. Preheat the oven to 425F and line a large rimmed baking sheet with parchment.
2. Spread the veggies on the baking sheet and drizzle with oil and vinegar.
3. Toss well and season with salt and pepper.
4. Spread the veggies in a single layer then roast for 20 to 25 minutes, stirring every 10 minutes, until tender.
5. Adjust seasoning to taste and serve hot.

Nutrition: Calories 100, Fat 5g, Carbs 12.4g, Protein 3.2g, Sugar 5.5g, Fiber 4.2g, Sodium 51mg

168. Parsley Tabbouleh

Preparation time: 5 minutes

Cooking Time: 25 minutes

Servings: 6

Ingredients:

- 1 cup water
- 1/2 cup bulgur
- ¼ cup fresh lemon juice
- 2 tablespoons olive oil
- 2 cloves minced garlic
- Salt and pepper
- 2 cups fresh chopped parsley

- 2 medium tomatoes, died
- 1 small cucumber, diced
- ¼ cup fresh chopped mint

Directions:

1. Bring the water and bulgur to a boil in a small saucepan then remove from heat.
2. Cover and let stand until the water is fully absorbed, about 25 minutes.
3. Meanwhile, whisk together the lemon juice, olive oil, garlic, salt, and pepper in a medium bowl.
4. Toss in the cooked bulgur along with the parsley, tomatoes, cucumber, and mint.
5. Season with salt and pepper to taste and serve.

Nutrition: Calories 110, Fat 5.3g, Carbs 14.4g, Protein 3g, Sugar 2.4g, Fiber 3.9g, Sodium 21mg

169. Garlic Sautéed Spinach

Preparation time: 5 minutes

Cooking Time: 10 minutes

Servings: 4

Ingredients:

- 1 1/2 tablespoons olive oil
- 4 cloves minced garlic
- 6 cups fresh baby spinach
- Salt and pepper

Directions:

1. Heat the oil in a large skillet over medium-high heat.

2. Add the garlic and cook for 1 minute.

3. Stir in the spinach and season with salt and pepper.

4. Sauté for 1 to 2 minutes until just wilted. Serve hot.

Nutrition: Calories 60, Fat 5.5g, Carbs 2.6g, Protein 1.5g, Sugar 0.2g, Fiber 1.1g, Sodium 36mg

170. French Lentils

Preparation time: 5 minutes

Cooking Time: 25 minutes

Servings: 10

Ingredients:

- 2 tablespoons olive oil

- 1 medium onion, diced

- 1 medium carrot, peeled and diced

- 2 cloves minced garlic

- 5 1/2 cups water

- 2 ¼ cups French lentils, rinsed and drained

- 1 teaspoon dried thyme

- 2 small bay leaves

- Salt and pepper

Directions:

1. Heat the oil in a large saucepan over medium heat.

2. Add the onions, carrot, and garlic and sauté for 3 minutes.

3. Stir in the water, lentils, thyme, and bay leaves: season with salt.

4. Bring to a boil then reduce to a simmer and cook until tender, about 20 minutes.

5. Drain any excess water and adjust seasoning to taste. Serve hot.

Nutrition: Calories 185, Fat 3.3g, Carbs 27.9g, Protein 11.4g, Sugar 1.7g, Fiber 13.7g, Sodium 11mg

171. Grain-Free Berry Cobbler

Preparation time: 5 minutes

Cooking Time: 25 minutes

Servings: 10

Ingredients:

- 4 cups fresh mixed berries

- 1/2 cup ground flaxseed

- ¼ cup almond meal

- ¼ cup unsweetened shredded coconut

- 1/2 tablespoon baking powder

- 1 teaspoon ground cinnamon

- ¼ teaspoon salt

- Powdered stevia, to taste

- 6 tablespoons coconut oil

Directions:

1. Preheat the oven to 375F and lightly grease a 10-inch cast-iron skillet.

2. Spread the berries on the bottom of the skillet.

3. Whisk together the dry ingredients in a mixing bowl.

4. Cut in the coconut oil using a fork to create a crumbled mixture.

5. Spread the crumble over the berries and bake for 25 minutes until hot and bubbling.

6. Cool the cobbler for 5 to 10 minutes before serving.

Nutrition: Calories 215 Fat 16.8g, Carbs 13.1g, Protein 3.7g, Sugar 5.3g, Fiber 6.4g, Sodium 61mg

172. Coffee-Steamed Carrots

Preparation Time: 10 minutes

Cooking Time: 3 minutes

Servings: 4

Ingredients:

- 1 cup brewed coffee

- 1 teaspoon light brown sugar

- ½ teaspoon kosher salt

- Freshly ground black pepper

- 1-pound baby carrots

- Chopped fresh parsley

- 1 teaspoon grated lemon zest

Directions:

1. Pour the coffee into the electric pressure cooker. Stir in the brown sugar, salt, and pepper. Add the carrots.

2. Close the pressure cooker. Set to sealing.

3. Cook on high pressure for minutes.

4. Once complete, click Cancel and quick release the pressure.

5. Once the pin drops, open and remove the lid.

6. Using a slotted spoon, portion carrots to a serving bowl. Topped with the parsley and lemon zest, and serve.

Nutrition: Calories: 48 Carbs: 11g Protein: 3g Sugar: 11g; Fiber: 10g; Sodium: 318mg

173. Rosemary Potatoes

Preparation Time: 5 minutes

Cooking Time: 25 minutes

Servings: 2

Ingredients:

- 1lb red potatoes

- 1 cup vegetable stock

- 2tbsp olive oil

- 2tbsp rosemary sprigs

Directions:

1. Situate potatoes in the steamer basket and add the stock into the Instant Pot.

2. Steam the potatoes in your Instant Pot for 15 minutes.

3. Depressurize and pour away the remaining stock.

4. Set to sauté and add the oil, rosemary, and potatoes.

5. Cook until brown.

Nutrition: Calories 171 Carbs 21g Protein 6.8g Sugar: 11g; Fiber: 9g; Sodium: 396mg

174. Vegetable Salad

Preparation time: 10 minutes

Cooking time: 0 minutes

Servings: 1-2

Ingredients:

• 4 cups each of raw spinach and romaine lettuce

• 2 cups each of cherry tomatoes, sliced cucumber, chopped baby carrots and chopped red, orange and yellow bell pepper

• 1 cup each of chopped broccoli, sliced yellow squash, zucchini and cauliflower.

Directions:

1. Wash all these vegetables.

2. Mix in a large mixing bowl and top off with a non-fat or low-fat dressing of your choice.

Nutrition: Calories: 48 Carbs: 11g Protein: 3g Sugar: 11g; Fiber: 10g; Sodium: 318mg

Dessert Recipes

175. Peanut Butter Cups

Preparation Time: 5 minutes

Cooking Time: 10 minutes

Servings: 4

Ingredients:

• 1 packet plain gelatin

• ¼ cup sugar substitute

• 2 cups nonfat cream

• ½ teaspoon vanilla

• ¼ cup low-fat peanut butter

• 2 tablespoons unsalted peanuts, chopped

Directions:

1. Mix gelatin, sugar substitute and cream in a pan.

2. Let sit for 5 minutes.

3. Place over medium heat and cook until gelatin has been dissolved.

4. Stir in vanilla and peanut butter.

5. Pour into custard cups. Chill for 3 hours.

6. Top with the peanuts and serve.

Nutrition: 171 Calories 21g Carbohydrate 6.8g Protein

176. Peanut Chocolate Fondue

Preparation time: 5 minutes

Cooking time: 10 minutes

Servings: 2

Ingredients:

• 1 cup water

• ½ tsp. sugar or stevia

• ½ cup coconut cream

• ¾ cup dark chocolate, chopped

Directions:

1. Pour the water into your Instant Pot.

2. To a heatproof bowl, add the chocolate, sugar, and coconut cream.

3. Place in the Instant Pot.

4. Seal the lid, select MANUAL, and cook for 2 minutes. When ready, do a quick release and

carefully open the lid. Stir well and serve immediately.

Nutrition: Calories: 216 Fat: 17 g Protein: 2 g Carbs: 11 g Fiber: 2.4 g Sugar: 16 g Sodium: 633 mg

177. Fruit Pizza

Preparation Time: 5 minutes

Cooking Time: 10 minutes

Servings: 4

Ingredients:

- 1 teaspoon maple syrup

- ¼ teaspoon vanilla extract

- ½ cup coconut milk yogurt

- 2 round slices watermelon

- ½ cup blackberries, sliced

- ½ cup strawberries, sliced

- 2 tablespoons coconut flakes (unsweetened)

Directions:

1. Mix maple syrup, vanilla and yogurt in a bowl.

2. Spread the mixture on top of the watermelon slice.

3. Top with the berries and coconut flakes.

Nutrition: Calories 70 Carbs 14.6g Protein 1.2g Sugar: 13.2g; Fiber: 9.4g; Sodium: 331mg

178. Choco Peppermint Cake

Preparation Time: 5 minutes

Cooking Time: 10 minutes

Servings: 4

Ingredients:

- Cooking spray

- 1/3 cup oil

- 15 oz. package chocolate cake mix

- 3 eggs, beaten

- 1 cup water

- ¼ teaspoon peppermint extract

Directions:

1. Spray slow cooker with oil.

2. Mix all the ingredients in a bowl.

3. Use an electric mixer on medium speed setting to mix ingredients for 2 minutes.

4. Pour mixture into the slow cooker.

5. Cover the pot and cook on low for 3 hours.

6. Let cool before slicing and serving.

Nutrition: Calories 102 Carbs 27g Protein 3.8g Sugar: 11g; Fiber: 9g; Sodium: 336mg

179. Roasted Plums

Preparation Time: 5 minutes

Cooking Time: 10 minutes

Servings: 4

Ingredients:

- Cooking spray

- 6 plums, sliced

- ½ cup pineapple juice (unsweetened)

- 1 tablespoon brown sugar

- 2 tablespoons brown sugar
- ¼ teaspoon ground cardamom
- ½ teaspoon ground cinnamon
- 1/8 teaspoon ground cumin

Directions:

1. Combine all the ingredients in a baking pan.

2. Roast in the oven at 450 degrees F for 20 minutes.

Nutrition: Calories 102 Carbs 18.7g Protein 2g Sugar: 11g; Sodium: 396mg Fiber: 9g;

180. Flourless Chocolate Cake

Preparation Time: 10 minutes

Cooking Time: 45 minutes

Servings: 6

Ingredients:

- ½ Cup of stevia
- 12 Ounces of unsweetened baking chocolate
- 2/3 Cup of ghee
- 1/3 Cup of warm water
- ¼ Teaspoon of salt
- 4 Large pastured eggs
- 2 Cups of boiling water

Directions:

1. Line the bottom of a 9-inch pan of a spring form with a parchment paper.

2. Heat the water in a small pot; then add the salt and the stevia over the water until wait until the mixture becomes completely dissolved.

3. Melt the baking chocolate into a double boiler or simply microwave it for about 30 seconds.

4. Mix the melted chocolate and the butter in a large bowl with an electric mixer.

5. Beat in your hot mixture; then crack in the egg and whisk after adding each of the eggs.

6. Pour the obtained mixture into your prepared spring form tray.

7. Wrap the spring form tray with a foil paper.

8. Place the spring form tray in a large cake tray and add boiling water right to the outside; make sure the depth doesn't exceed 1 inch.

9. Bake the cake into the water bath for about 45 minutes at a temperature of about 350 F.

10. Remove the tray from the boiling water and transfer to a wire to cool.

11. Let the cake chill for an overnight in the refrigerator.

Nutrition: Calories 295 Carbs 6g Fiber 4g Sodium: 319mg Protein: 15g; Sugar: 11g;

181. Lava Cake

Preparation Time: 10 minutes

Cooking Time: 10 minutes

Servings: 2

Ingredients:

- 2 Oz of dark chocolate; you should at least use chocolate of 85% cocoa solids
- 1 Tablespoon of super-fine almond flour

- 2 Oz of unsalted almond butter

- 2 Large eggs

Directions:

1.   Heat your oven to a temperature of about 350 Fahrenheit.

2.   Grease 2 heat proof ramekins with almond butter.

3.   Now, melt the chocolate and the almond butter and stir very well.

4.   Beat the eggs very well with a mixer.

5.   Add the eggs to the chocolate and the butter mixture and mix very well with almond flour and the swerve; then stir.

6.   Pour the dough into 2 ramekins.

7.   Bake for about 9 to 10 minutes.

8.   Turn the cakes over plates and serve with pomegranate seeds!

Nutrition: Calories 459 Carbs 3.5g Fiber 0.8g Protein: 15g; Sugar: 11g; Sodium: 273mg

182.   Pretzels

Preparation Time: 10 minutes

Cooking Time: 20 minutes

Servings: 8

Ingredients:

- 1 and ½ cups of pre-shredded mozzarella

- 2 Tablespoons of full fat cream cheese

- 1 Large egg

- ¾ Cup of almond flour+ 2 tablespoons of ground almonds or almond meal

- ½ Teaspoon of baking powder

- 1 Pinch of coarse sea salt

Directions:

1.   Heat your oven to a temperature of about 180 C/356 F.

2.   Melt the cream cheese and the mozzarella cheese and stir over a low heat until the cheeses are perfectly melted.

3.   If you choose to microwave the cheese, just do that for about 1 minute no more and if you want to do it on the stove, turn off the heat as soon as the cheese is completely melted.

4.   Add the large egg to the prepared warm dough; then stir until your ingredients are very well combined. If the egg is cold; you will need to heat it gently.

5.   Add in the ground almonds or the almond flour and the baking powder and stir until your ingredients are very well combined.

6.   Take one pinch of the dough of cheese and toll it or stretch it in your hands until it is about 18 to 20 cm of length; if your dough is sticky, you can oil your hands to avoid that.

7.   Now, form pretzels from the cheese dough and nicely shape it; then place it over a baking sheet.

8.   Sprinkle with a little bit of salt and bake for about 17 minutes.

Nutrition: Calories 113 Carbs 2.5g Fiber 0.8g Protein: 11g; Sugar: 12g; Sodium: 314mg

183.   Cheesy Taco Bites

Preparation Time: 5 minutes

Cooking Time: 10minutes

Serving: 12

Ingredients

- 2 Cups of Packaged Shredded Cheddar Cheese

- 2 Tablespoon of Chili Powder

- 2 Tablespoons of Cumin

- 1 Teaspoon of Salt

- 8 Teaspoons of coconut cream for garnishing

- Use Pico de Gallo for garnishing as well

Directions:

1.	Preheat your oven to a temperature of about 350 F.

2.	Over a baking sheet lined with a parchment paper, place 1 tablespoon piles of cheese and make sure to a space of 2 inches between each.

3.	Place the baking sheet in your oven and bake for about 5 minutes.

4.	Remove from the oven and let the cheese cool down for about 1 minute; then carefully lift up and press each into the cups of a mini muffin tin.

5.	Make sure to press the edges of the cheese to form the shape of muffins mini.

6.	Let the cheese cool completely; then remove it.

7.	While you continue to bake the cheese and create your cups.

8.	Fill the cheese cups with the coconut cream, then top with the Pico de Gallo.

Nutrition: Calories 73 Carbs 3g Protein 4g Sugar: 11g; Fiber: 9g; Sodium: 237mg

184.   Nut Squares

Preparation Time: 30 minutes

Cooking Time: 10 minutes

Serving: 10

Ingredients:

- 2 Cups of almonds, pumpkin seeds, sunflower seeds and walnuts

- ½ Cup of desiccated coconut

- 1 Tablespoon of chia seeds

- ¼ Teaspoon of salt

- 2 Tablespoons of coconut oil

- 1 Teaspoon of vanilla extract

- 3 Tablespoons of almond or peanut butter

- 1/3 Cup of Sukrin Gold Fiber Syrup

Directions:

1.	Line a square baking tin with a baking paper; then lightly grease it with cooking spray

2.	Chop all the nuts roughly; then slightly grease it too, you can also leave them as whole

3.	Mix the nuts in a large bowl; then combine them in a large bowl with the coconut, the chia seeds and the salt

4.	In a microwave-proof bowl; add the coconut oil; then add the vanilla, the coconut butter or oil, the almond butter and the fiber syrup and microwave the mixture for about 30 seconds

5.	Stir your ingredients together very well; then pour the melted mixture right on top of the nuts

6.	Press the mixture into your prepared baking tin with the help of the back of a measuring cup and push very well

7. Freeze your treat for about 1 hour before cutting it

8. Cut your frozen nut batter into small cubes or squares of the same size

Nutrition: Calories 268 Carbs 14g Fiber 1g Protein: 18g; Sugar: 11g; Sodium: 329mg

185. Pumpkin & Banana Ice Cream

Preparation Time: 5 minutes

Cooking Time: 10 minutes

Servings: 4

Ingredients:

- 15 oz. pumpkin puree

- 4 bananas, sliced and frozen

- 1 teaspoon pumpkin pie spice

- Chopped pecans

Directions:

1. Add pumpkin puree, bananas and pumpkin pie spice in a food processor.

2. Pulse until smooth.

3. Chill in the refrigerator.

4. Garnish with pecans.

Nutrition: Calories 71 Carbs 18g Protein 1.2g Sugar: 11g; Fiber: 9g; Sodium: 396mg

186. Brulee Oranges

Preparation Time: 5 minutes

Cooking Time: 10 minutes

Servings: 4

Ingredients:

- 4 oranges, sliced into segments

- 1 teaspoon ground cardamom

- 6 teaspoons brown sugar

- 1 cup nonfat Greek yogurt

Directions:

1. Preheat your broiler.

2. Arrange orange slices in a baking pan.

3. In a bowl, mix the cardamom and sugar.

4. Sprinkle mixture on top of the oranges. Broil for 5 minutes.

5. Serve oranges with yogurt.

Nutrition: Calories 168 Carbs 26.9g Protein 6.8g Sugar: 13g; Fiber: 19g; Sodium: 221mg

187. Frozen Lemon & Blueberry

Preparation Time: 5 minutes

Cooking Time: 10 minutes

Servings: 4

Ingredients:

- 6 cup fresh blueberries

- 8 sprigs fresh thyme

- ¾ cup light brown sugar

- 1 teaspoon lemon zest

- ¼ cup lemon juice

- 2 cups water

Directions:

1. Add blueberries, thyme and sugar in a pan over medium heat.

2. Cook for 6 to 8 minutes.

3. Transfer mixture to a blender.

4. Remove thyme sprigs.

5. Stir in the remaining ingredients.

6. Pulse until smooth.

7. Strain mixture and freeze for 1 hour.

Nutrition: Calories 78 Carbs 20g Protein 3g Sugar: 21g; Fiber: 12g; Sodium: 391mg

188. Peanut Butter Choco Chip Cookies

Preparation Time: 5 minutes

Cooking Time: 10 minutes

Servings: 4

Ingredients:

- 1 egg

- ½ cup light brown sugar

- 1 cup natural unsweetened peanut butter

- Pinch salt

- ¼ cup dark chocolate chips

Directions:

1. Preheat your oven to 375 degrees F.

2. Mix egg, sugar, peanut butter, salt and chocolate chips in a bowl.

3. Form into cookies and place in a baking pan.

4. Bake the cookie for 10 minutes.

5. Let cool before serving.

Nutrition: Calories 159 Carbs 12g Protein 4.3g Sugar: 11g; Fiber: 9g; Sodium: 313mg

189. Watermelon Sherbet

Preparation Time: 5 minutes

Cooking Time: 3 minutes

Servings: 4

Ingredients:

- 6 cups watermelon, sliced into cubes

- 14 oz. almond milk

- 1 tablespoon honey

- ¼ cup lime juice

- Salt to taste

Directions:

1. Freeze watermelon for 4 hours.

2. Add frozen watermelon and other ingredients in a blender.

3. Blend until smooth.

4. Transfer to a container with seal.

5. Seal and freeze for 4 hours.

Nutrition: 132 Calories 24.5g Carbohydrate 3.1g Protein

190. Strawberry & Mango Ice Cream

Preparation Time: 5 minutes

Cooking Time: 10 minutes

Servings: 4

Ingredients:

- 8 oz. strawberries, sliced

- 12 oz. mango, sliced into cubes

- 1 tablespoon lime juice

Directions:

1. Add all ingredients in a food processor.

2. Pulse for 2 minutes.

3. Chill before serving.

Nutrition: Calories 70 Carbs 17.4g Protein 11g; Sugar: 12.1g Fiber: 15g; Sodium: 292mg

191. Sparkling Fruit Drink

Preparation Time: 5 minutes

Cooking Time: 10 minutes

Servings: 4

Ingredients:

- 8 oz. unsweetened grape juice

- 8 oz. unsweetened apple juice

- 8 oz. unsweetened orange juice

- 1 qt. homemade ginger ale

- Ice

Directions:

1. 1.Makes 7 servings. Mix first 4 ingredients together in a pitcher. Stir in ice cubes and 9 ounces of the beverage to each glass. Serve immediately.

Nutrition: Calories 60 Protein 1.1g Carbs: 71g; Sodium: 396mg Sugar: 11g; Fiber: 9g;

192. Tiramisu Shots

Preparation Time: 5 minutes

Cooking Time: 10 minutes

Servings: 4

Ingredients:

- 1 pack silken tofu

- 1 oz. dark chocolate, finely chopped

- ¼ cup sugar substitute

- 1 teaspoon lemon juice

- ¼ cup brewed espresso

- Pinch salt

- 24 slices angel food cake

- Cocoa powder (unsweetened)

Directions:

1. Add tofu, chocolate, sugar substitute, lemon juice, espresso and salt in a food processor.

2. Pulse until smooth.

3. Add angel food cake pieces into shot glasses.

4. Drizzle with the cocoa powder.

5. Pour the tofu mixture on top.

6. Top with the remaining angel food cake pieces.

7. Chill for 30 minutes and serve.

Nutrition: Calories 75 Carbs 12g Protein 2.9g Sugar: 9g; Fiber: 18g; Sodium: 272mg

193. Ice Cream Brownie Cake

Preparation Time: 5 minutes

Cooking Time: 10 minutes

Servings: 4

Ingredients:

- Cooking spray

- 12 oz. no-sugar brownie mix

- ¼ cup oil

- 2 egg whites

- 3 tablespoons water

- 2 cups sugar-free ice cream

Directions:

1.   Preheat your oven to 325 degrees F.

2.   Spray your baking pan with oil.

3.   Mix brownie mix, oil, egg whites and water in a bowl.

4.   Pour into the baking pan.

5.   Bake for 25 minutes.

6.   Let cool.

7.   Freeze brownie for 2 hours.

8.   Spread ice cream over the brownie.

9.   Freeze for 8 hours.

Nutrition: Calories 198 Carbs 33g Protein 3g Sugar: 11g; Fiber: 9g; Sodium: 256mg

194.   Berry Sorbet

Preparation time: 10 minutes

Cooking time: 20 minutes

Servings: 6

Ingredients:

- Water, 2 c

- Blend strawberries, 2 c

- Spelt Flour, 1.5 tsp.

- Date sugar, .5 c

Directions:

1.   Add the water into a large pot and let the water begin to warm. Add the flour and date sugar and stir until dissolved. Allow this mixture to start boiling and continue to cook for

around ten minutes. It should have started to thicken. Take off the heat and set to the side to cool.

2.   Once the syrup has cooled off, add in the strawberries, and stir well to combine.

3.   Pour into a container that is freezer safe and put it into the freezer until frozen.

4.   Take sorbet out of the freezer, cut into chunks, and put it either into a blender or a food processor. Hit the pulse button until the mixture is creamy.

5.   Pour this into the same freezer-safe container and put it back into the freezer for four hours.

Nutrition: Calories: 99 Carbs: 8 g Protein: 15g; Sugar: 11g; Fiber: 9g; Sodium: 396mg

195.   Quinoa Porridge

Preparation time: 5 minutes

Cooking time: 15 minutes

Servings: 04

Ingredients:

- Zest of one lime

- Coconut milk, .5 c

- Cloves, .5 tsp.

- Ground ginger, 1.5 tsp.

- Spring water, 2 c

- Quinoa, 1 c

- Grated apple, 1

Directions:

1.   Cook the quinoa. Follow the instructions on the package. When the quinoa has been cooked, drain well. Place it back into the pot and stir in spices.

2. Add coconut milk and stir well to combine.

3. Grate the apple now and stir well.

4. Divide equally into bowls and add the lime zest on top. Sprinkle with nuts and seeds of choice.

Nutrition: Calories: 180 Fat: 3 g Carbs: 40 g Protein: 10 g Sugar: 10g; Fiber: 19g; Sodium: 322mg

196. Apple Quinoa

Preparation time: 15 minutes

Cooking time: 30 minutes

Servings: 04

Ingredients:

- Coconut oil, 1 tbsp.

- Ginger

- Key lime.5

- Apple, 1

- Quinoa,.5 c

- Optional toppings

- Seeds

- Nuts

- Berries

Directions:

1. Fix the quinoa according to the instructions on the package. When you are getting close to the end of the **Cooking time**, grate in the apple and cook for 30 seconds.

2. Zest the lime into the quinoa and squeeze the juice in. Stir in the coconut oil.

3. Divide evenly into bowls and sprinkle with some ginger.

4. You can add in some berries, nuts, and seeds right before you eat.

Nutrition: Calories: 146 Fiber: 2.3 g Fat: 8.3 g Protein: 17g; Carbs: 71g; Sugar: 13g; Sodium: 381mg

197. Kamut Porridge

Preparation time: 10 minutes

Cooking time: 25 minutes

Servings: 04

Ingredients:

- Agave syrup, 4 tbsp.

- Coconut oil, 1 tbsp.

- Sea salt,.5 tsp.

- Coconut milk, 3.75 c

- Kamut berries, 1 c

- Optional toppings

- Berries

- Coconut chips

- Ground nutmeg

- Ground cloves

Directions:

1. You need to "crack" the Kamut berries. You can try this by placing the berries into a food processor and pulsing until you have 1.25 cups of Kamut.

2. Place the cracked Kamut in a pot with salt and coconut milk. Give it a good stir in order to combine everything. Allow this mixture to come to a full rolling boil and then turn the heat down until the mixture is simmering. Stir

every now and then until the Kamut has thickened to your likeness. This normally takes about ten minutes.

3.   Take off heat, stir in agave syrup and coconut oil.

4.   Garnish with toppings of choice and enjoy.

Nutrition: Calories: 114 Protein: 5 g Fat: 8.3 g Carbs: 24g Fiber: 4 g: 11g; Sodium: 383mg

198.   Hot Kamut With Peaches, Walnuts, And Coconut

Preparation time: 10 minutes

Cooking time: 35 minutes

Servings: 04

Ingredients:

*   Toasted coconut, 4 tbsp.

*   Toasted and chopped walnuts,.5 c

*   Chopped dried peaches, 8

*   Coconut milk, 3 c

*   Kamut cereal, 1 c

Directions:

1.   Mix the coconut milk into a saucepan and allow it to warm up. When it begins simmering, add in the Kamut. Let this cook about 15 minutes, while stirring every now and then.

2.   When done, divide evenly into bowls and top with the toasted coconut, walnuts, and peaches.

3.   You could even go one more and add some fresh berries.

Nutrition: Calories: 156 Protein: 5.8 g Fat: 7.5 g Carbs: 25 g Fiber: 6 g Sugar: 11g; Sodium: 396mg

199.   Overnight "Oats"

Preparation time: 5 minutes

Cooking time: 0 minutes

Servings: 04

Ingredients:

*   Berry of choice,.5 c

*   Walnut butter,.5 tbsp.

*   Burro banana,.5

*   Ginger,.5 tsp.

*   Coconut milk,.5 c

*   Hemp seeds,.5 c

Directions:

1.   Put the hemp seeds, salt, and coconut milk into a glass jar. Mix well.

2.   Place the lid on the jar then put in the refrigerator to sit overnight.

3.   The next morning, add the ginger, berries, and banana. Stir well and enjoy.

Nutrition: Calories: 139 Fat: 4.1 g Protein: 9 g Sugar: 7 g Carbs: 15g Fiber: 12g; Sodium: 283mg

200.   Blueberry Cupcakes

Preparation time: 15 minutes

Cooking time: 40 minutes

Servings: 04

Ingredients:

*   Grapeseed oil

*   Sea salt,.5 tsp.

*   Sea moss gel,.25 c

- Agave, .3 c

- Blueberries, .5 c

- Teff flour, .75 c

- Spelt flour, .75 c

- Coconut milk, 1 c

Directions:

1.   Warm your oven to 365. Place paper liners into a muffin tin.

2.   Place sea moss gel, sea salt, agave, flour, and milk in large bowl. Mix well to combine. Gently fold in blueberries.

3.   Gently pour batter into paper liners. Place in oven and bake 30 minutes.

4.   They are done if they have turned a nice golden color, and they spring back when you touch them.

Nutrition: Calories: 85 Fat: 0.7 g Carbs: 12 g Protein: 1.4 g Fiber: 5 g Sugar: 11g; Sodium: 686mg

Chapter 6: Recipe index

Beet Salad with Basil Dressing	125
Berry Apple Cider	103
Berry Sorbet	156
Berry-oat breakfast bars	33
Blackened Shrimp	119
Blueberry and Chicken Salad	102
Blueberry breakfast cake	35
Blueberry Buns	93
Blueberry Crisp	163
Blueberry Cupcakes	159
Blueberry Lemon Custard Cake	161
Braised Shrimp	115
Braised Summer Squash	137
Brazil Nut Cheese	159
Breakfast Smoothie Bowl with Fresh Berries	45
Broccoli Salad	132
Brown Rice & Lentil Salad	138
Brulee Oranges	153
Brunswick Stew	103
Bruschetta	92
Brussels Sprouts	133
Buckwheat grouts breakfast bowl	30
Buffalo Chicken Salads	104
C	
Cacciatore Style Chicken	104
Cajun Catfish	119

Cajun Flounder & Tomatoes	120
Cajun Shrimp & Roasted Vegetables	120
Caprese Turkey Burgers	60
Carnitas Tacos	105
Carrot Hummus	135
Cauliflower Mac & Cheese	72
Cauliflower Muffin	69
Cauliflower Potato Mash	93
Cauliflower Rice with Chicken	48
Cheese Cake	148
Cheesy Cauliflower Gratin	90
Cheesy Low-Carb Omelet	38
Cheesy Salmon Fillets	84
Cheesy Taco Bites	151
Chia and Coconut Pudding	46
Chicken and Cornmeal Dumplings	107
Chicken and Pepperoni	108
Chicken and Roasted Vegetable Wraps	82
Chicken and Sausage Gumbo	108
Chicken Chili	106
Chicken Salad with Grapes and Pecans	53
Chicken Vera Cruz	106
Chicken with Caprese Salsa	66
Chicken, Barley, and Leek Stew	109
Chicken, Strawberry, And Avocado Salad	62
Chili Lime Salmon	143

Chipotle Chili Pork Chops	78
Chipotle Lettuce Chicken	42
Choco Peppermint Cake	145
Chocolate Quinoa Brownies	163
Cider Pork Stew	109
Cilantro Lime Drumsticks	134
Cilantro Lime Grilled Shrimp	121
Cilantro Lime Quinoa	138
Cinnamon and Coconut Porridge	37
Citrus Salmon	113
Cobb Salad	87
Coconut-Lentil Curry	51
Coffee-and-Herb-Marinated Steak	81
Coffee-Steamed Carrots	141
Collard Greens	143
Corn on the Cob	142
Courgettes In Cider Sauce	57
Crab Curry	112
Crab Frittata	121
Cranberry And Brussels Sprouts With Dressing	127
Cream Buns with Strawberries	92
Creamed Spinach	74
Creamy Chicken Noodle Soup	110
Creamy Taco Soup	66
Cuban Pulled Pork Sandwich	110
Curry Roasted Cauliflower Florets	136

Hearty Beef and Vegetable Soup	68
Herbed Salmon	114
Homestyle Herb Meatballs	79
Hot Kamut With Peaches, Walnuts, And Coconut	158
I	
Ice Cream Brownie Cake	156
Italian Beef	99
K	
Kale Pesto's Pasta	124
Kamut Porridge	157
L	
Lamb with Broccoli & Carrots	99
Lava Cake	148
Lean Lamb and Turkey Meatballs with Yogurt	83
Lemon Garlic Green Beans	137
Lemon Pepper Salmon	118
Lemon Sole	117
Lemon-Thyme Eggs	63
Lemony Salmon	117
Lemony Salmon Burgers	59
Lighter Eggplant Parmesan	50
Lighter Shrimp Scampi	52
Lime-Parsley Lamb Cutlets	79
Lovely Porridge	35
M	
Madeleine	149

Peach muesli bake	31
Peanut Butter Choco Chip Cookies	154
Peanut Butter Cups	145
Pork Chop Diane	76
Pork Chops with Grape Sauce	98
Pork with Cranberry Relish	94
Pretzels	151
Pumpkin & Banana Ice Cream	153
Pumpkin Custard	160
Q	
Quick Low-Carb Oatmeal	44
Quinoa Porridge	156
R	
Roasted Beef with Peppercorn Sauce	80
Roasted Mango	146
Roasted Plums	146
Roasted Pork & Apples	94
Roasted Portobello Salad	131
Roasted Vegetables	54
Rosemary Lamb	100
Rosemary Potatoes	142
S	
Salmon in Green Sauce	114
Salmon with Asparagus	85
Salty Macadamia Chocolate Smoothie	30
Sardine Curry	116

Sautéed Apples and Onions	55
Scallion Sandwich	83
Seared Tuna Steak	88
Sesame Pork with Mustard Sauce	95
Shredded Chicken Salad	131
Shrimp Coconut Curry	115
Shrimp in Garlic Butter	86
Shrimp with Green Beans	112
Slow Cooker Peaches	160
Slow Cooker Two-Bean Sloppy Joes	49
Spanish Stew	65
Sparkling Fruit Drink	155
Spiced Okra	58
Spicy Chicken Cacciatore	82
Spicy Jalapeno Popper Deviled Eggs	34
Spinach & Orange Salad with Oil Drizzle	126
Spinach and cheese quiche	34
Spinach Salad with Bacon	63
Steak with Mushroom Sauce	95
Steak with Tomato & Herbs	96
Steamed Kale with Mediterranean Dressing	47
Steel-cut oatmeal bowl with fruit and nuts	31
Strawberry & Mango Ice Cream	154
Strawberry Spinach Salad	90
Stuffed Mushrooms	75
Stuffed Portobello with Cheese	51

Chapter 7: Meal Plan

28 DAYS	BREAKFAST	LUNCH	DINNER
Day 1	Bacon and Chicken Garlic Wrap	Cauliflower Rice with Chicken	Cauliflower Mac & Cheese
Day 2	Salty Macadamia Chocolate Smoothie	Turkey with Fried Eggs	Easy Egg Salad
Day 3	Buckwheat grouts breakfast bowl	Sweet Potato, Kale, and White Bean Stew	Baked Chicken Legs
Day 4	Peach muesli bake	Slow Cooker Two-Bean Sloppy Joes	Creamed Spinach
Day 5	Steel-cut oatmeal bowl with fruit and nuts	Lighter Eggplant Parmesan	Stuffed Mushrooms
Day 6	Whole-grain dutch baby pancake	Coconut-Lentil Curry	Vegetable Soup
Day 7	Mushroom, zucchini, and onion frittata	Stuffed Portobello with Cheese	Pork Chop Diane
Day 8	Berry-oat breakfast bars	Lighter Shrimp Scampi	Autumn Pork Chops with Red Cabbage and Apples
Day 9	Spinach and cheese quiche	Maple-Mustard Salmon	Chipotle Chili Pork Chops
Day 10	Spicy Jalapeno Popper Deviled Eggs	Chicken Salad with Grapes and Pecans	Orange-Marinated Pork Tenderloin
Day 11	Blueberry breakfast cake	Roasted Vegetables	Homestyle Herb Meatballs
Day 12	Lovely Porridge	Millet Pilaf	Lime-Parsley Lamb Cutlets
Day 13	Basil and Tomato Baked Eggs	Sweet and Sour Onions	Mediterranean Steak Sandwiches
Day 14	Whole-grain pancakes	Sautéed Apples and Onions	Roasted Beef with Peppercorn Sauce

Day 15	Whole-grain breakfast cookies	Zucchini Noodles with Portabella Mushrooms	Coffee-and-Herb-Marinated Steak
Day 16	Cinnamon and Coconut Porridge	Grilled Tempeh with Pineapple	Traditional Beef Stroganoff
Day 17	An Omelet of Swiss chard	Courgettes In Cider Sauce	Chicken and Roasted Vegetable Wraps
Day 18	Cheesy Low-Carb Omelet	Baked Mixed Mushrooms	Spicy Chicken Cacciatore
Day 19	Yogurt and Kale Smoothie	Spiced Okra	Scallion Sandwich
Day 20	Grilled Chicken Platter	Lemony Salmon Burgers	Lean Lamb and Turkey Meatballs with Yogurt
Day 21	Parsley Chicken Breast	Caprese Turkey Burgers	Air Fried Section and Tomato
Day 22	Mustard Chicken	Pasta Salad	Cheesy Salmon Fillets
Day 23	Balsamic Chicken	Chicken, Strawberry, And Avocado Salad	Salmon with Asparagus
Day 24	Greek Chicken Breast	Lemon-Thyme Eggs	Shrimp in Garlic Butter
Day 25	Chipotle Lettuce Chicken	Spinach Salad with Bacon	Cobb Salad
Day 26	Stylish Chicken-Bacon Wrap	Pea and Collards Soup	Seared Tuna Steak
Day 27	Healthy Cottage Cheese Pancakes	Spanish Stew	Beef Chili
Day 28	Avocado Lemon Toast	Creamy Taco Soup	Greek Broccoli Salad

Conclusion

Diabetes is a life-threatening disease caused by a lack of insulin. Insulin is a hormone that is required for the body's healthy functioning. The cells in a person's body do not respond to insulin effectively when they acquire diabetes. As a result, the cells does not get the energy and nutrients they require, and they begin to die.

Being diagnosed with diabetes will bring some major changes in your lifestyle. From the time you are diagnosed with it, it would always be a constant battle with food. You need to become a lot more careful with your food choices and the quantity that you ate. Every meal will feel like a major effort. You will be planning every day for the whole week, well in advance. Depending upon the type of food you ate, you have to keep checking your blood sugar levels. You may get used to taking long breaks between meals and staying away from snacks between dinner and breakfast.

Food would be treated as a bomb like it can go off at any time. According to an old saying, "When the body gets too hot, then your body heads straight to the kitchen."

Managing diabetes can be a very, very stressful ordeal. There will be many times that you will mark your glucose levels down on a piece of paper like you are plotting graph lines or something. You will mix your insulin shots up and then stress about whether or not you are giving yourself the right dosage. You will always be over-cautious because it involves a LOT of math and a really fine margin of error. But now, those days are gone!

With the help of technology and books, you can stock your kitchen with the right foods, like meal plans, diabetic friendly dishes, etc. You can also get an app that will even do the work for you. You can also people-watch on the internet and find the know-how to cook and eat right; you will always be a few meals away from certain disasters, like a plummeting blood sugar level. Always carry some sugar in your pocket. You won't have to experience the pangs of hunger but if you are unlucky, you will have to ration your food and bring along some simple low-calorie snacks with you.

This is the future of diabetes.

As you've reached the end of this book, you have gained complete control of your diabetes and this is where your expedition towards a better, healthier life starts. I hope I was able to inculcate some knowledge into you and make this adventure a little bit less of a struggle.

I would like to remind you that you're not alone in having to manage this disease and that nearly 85% of the new cases are 20 years old or younger.

Regardless of the length or seriousness of your diabetes, it can be managed! Take the information presented here and start with it!

Preparation is key to having a healthier and happier life.

It's helpful to remember that every tool at your disposal can help in some way.

Made in the USA
Monee, IL
28 October 2022

16750677R00079